STAR WARS®

BLOOD TIES

JANGO AND BOBA FETT

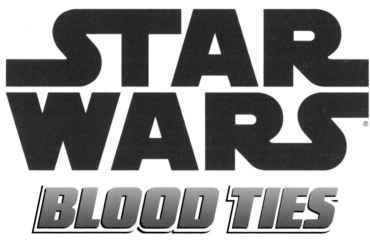

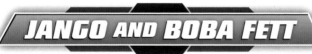

THE RISE OF THE EMPIRE
(1,000–0 years before the battle of Yavin)

After the seeming final defeat of the Sith, the Republic enters a state of complacency. In the waning years of the Republic, the Senate is rife with corruption, and the ambitious Senator Palpatine causes himself to be elected Supreme Chancellor. This is the era of the prequel trilogy.

The events in this story take place approximately twenty-two years before the Battle of Yavin.

STAR WARS®
BLOOD TIES
JANGO AND BOBA FETT

Script
TOM TAYLOR

Art
CHRIS SCALF

Letters
MICHAEL HEISLER

Cover Art
CHRIS SCALF

DARK HORSE BOOKS®

president and publisher
MIKE RICHARDSON

collection designer
STEPHEN REICHERT

editor
RANDY STRADLEY

assistant editor
FREDDYE LINS

NEIL HANKERSON executive vice president TOM WEDDLE chief financial officer RANDY STRADLEY vice president of publishing MICHAEL MARTENS vice president of business development ANITA NELSON vice president of business affairs MICHA HERSHMAN vice president of marketing DAVID SCROGGY vice president of product development DALE LAFOUNTAIN vice president of information technology DARLENE VOGEL director of purchasing KEN LIZZI general counsel DAVEY ESTRADA editorial director SCOTT ALLIE senior managing editor CHRIS WARNER senior books editor DIANA SCHUTZ executive editor CARY GRAZZINI director of design and production LIA RIBACCHI art director CARA NIECE director of scheduling

special thanks to Jann Moorhead, David Anderman, Troy Alders, Leland Chee,
Sue Rostoni, and Carol Roeder at Lucas Licensing

STAR WARS: BLOOD TIES Jango and Boba Fett

THIS VOLUME COLLECTS ISSUES #1–#4 OF THE DARK HORSE COMIC-BOOK SERIES
STAR WARS: BLOOD TIES—JANGO AND BOBA FETT.

PUBLISHED BY
DARK HORSE BOOKS
A DIVISION OF DARK HORSE COMICS, INC.
10956 SE MAIN STREET
MILWAUKIE, OR 97222

DarkHorse.com
StarWars.com

To find a comics shop in your area, call the Comic Shop Locator Service toll-free at 1-888-266-4226.

First edition: May 2011
ISBN 978-1-59582-627-5

1 3 5 7 9 10 8 6 4 2
Printed by Midas Printing International, Ltd., Huizhou, China.

Blood will out. The bonds of family—or the breaking of those bonds—affect the course of history. Wars have been fought, governments have fallen, and tragedy has been averted because of one person's blood relation with another.

Though not actually father and son, Jango Fett and Boba Fett share the same blood—literally. Boba will discover that the decisions made in Jango's life have an impact long after his death.

One of Jango's acts in particular is about to have a powerful impact. Something that begins when Boba is a child, while training with his father, is destined to continue when circumstances bring the past to the present . . . and to the attention of Boba Fett . . .

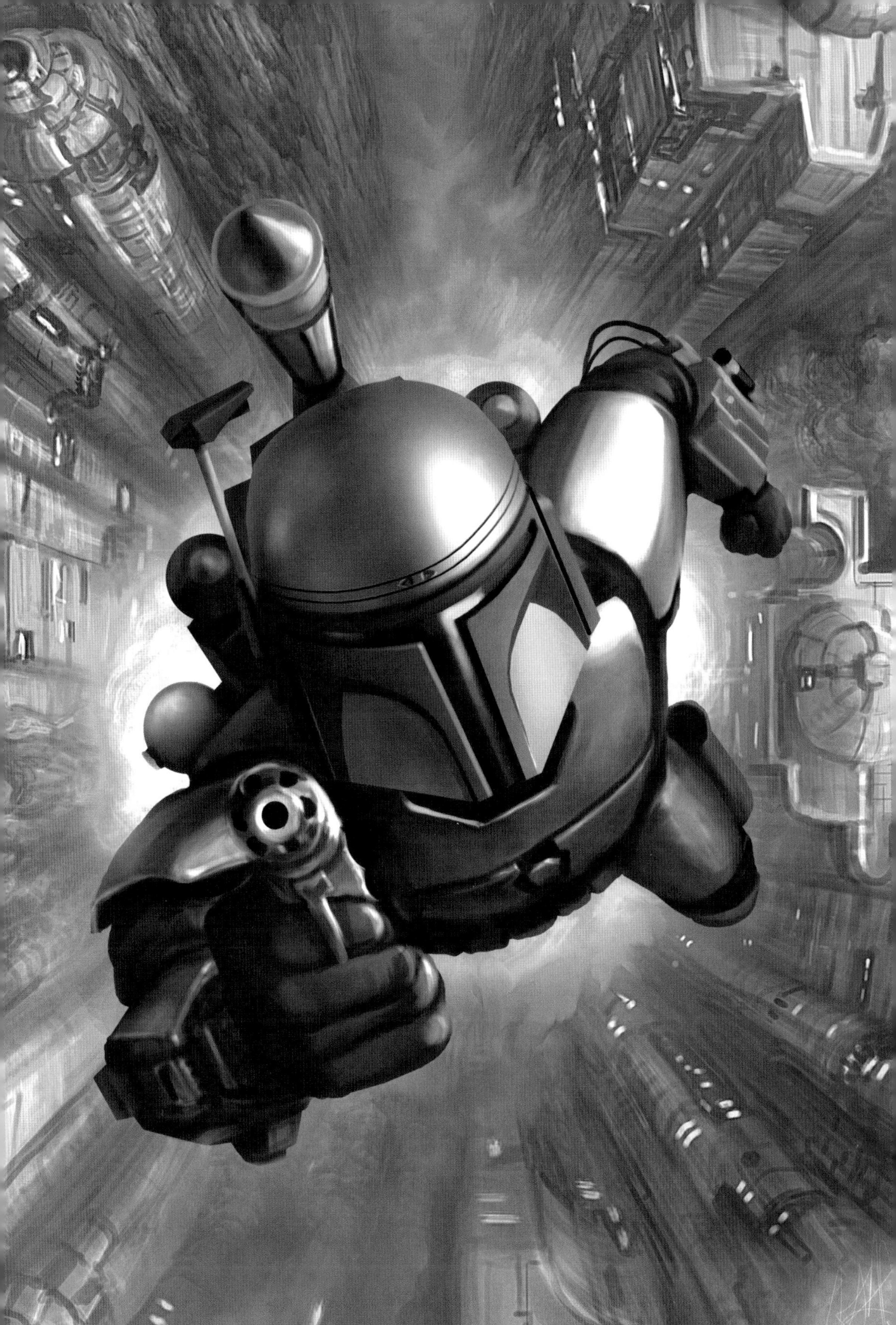

Illustration by
CHRIS SCALF

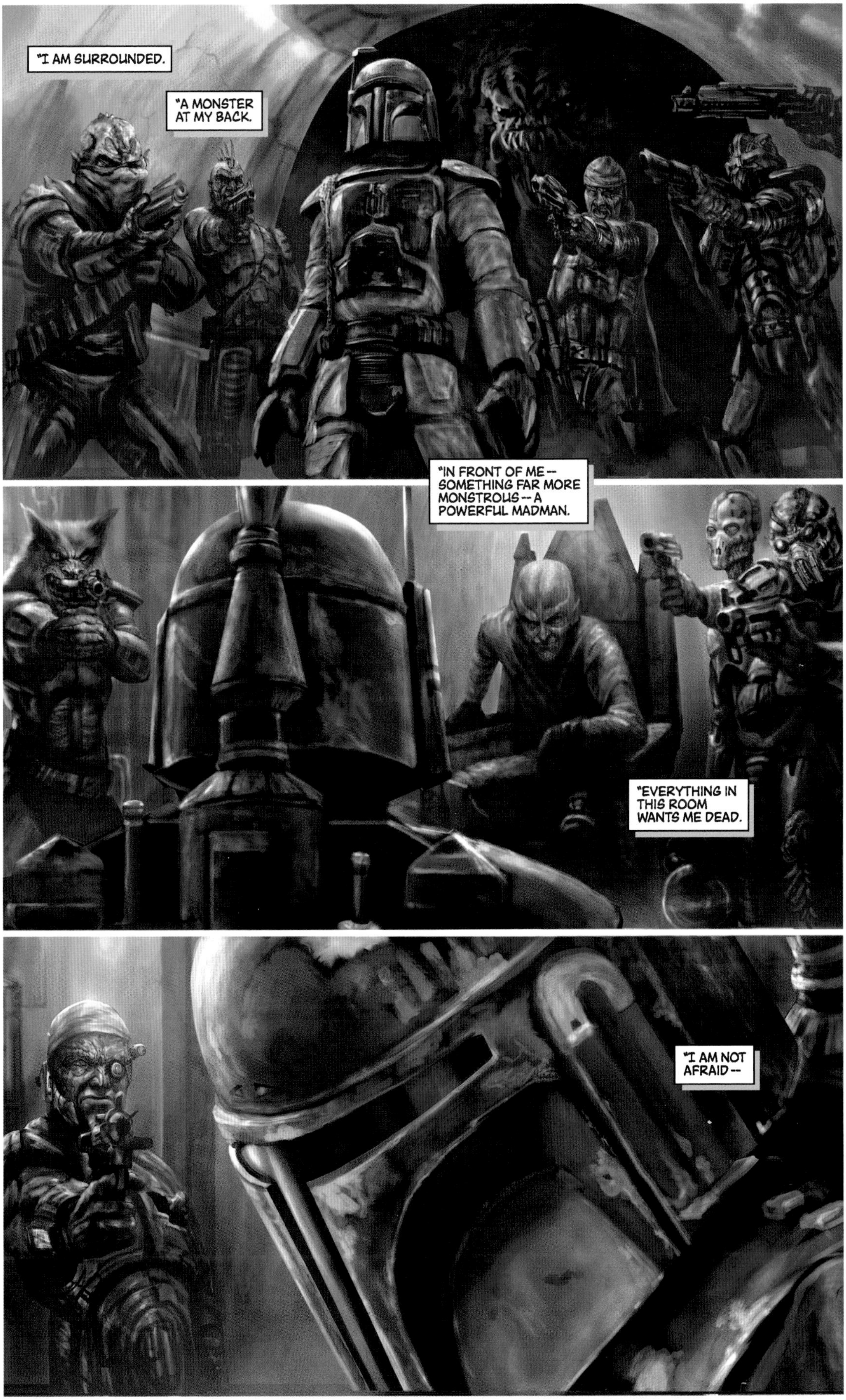

"I AM SURROUNDED.
"A MONSTER AT MY BACK.
"IN FRONT OF ME -- SOMETHING FAR MORE MONSTROUS -- A POWERFUL MADMAN.
"EVERYTHING IN THIS ROOM WANTS ME DEAD.
"I AM NOT AFRAID --

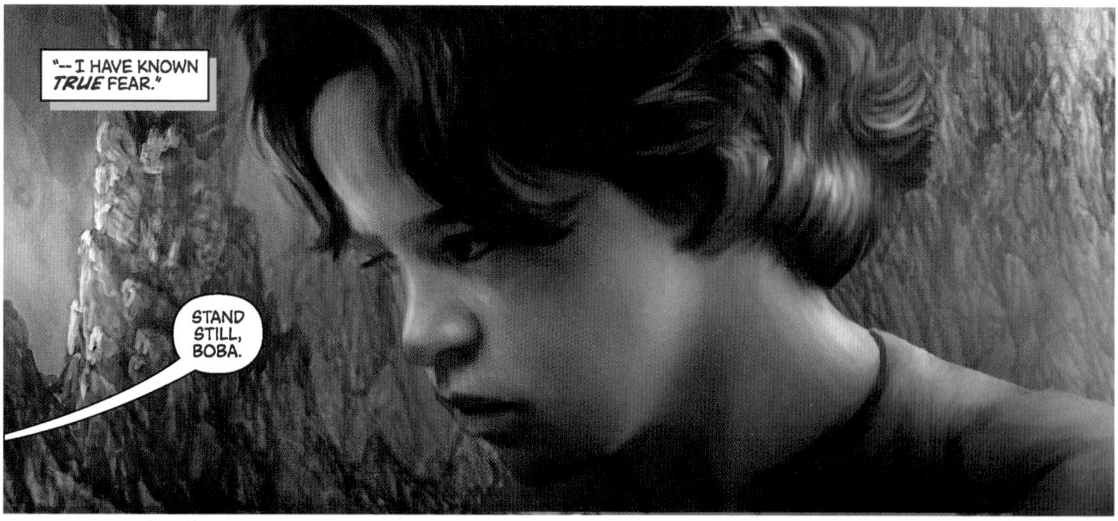
"-- I HAVE KNOWN *TRUE* FEAR."
STAND STILL, BOBA.

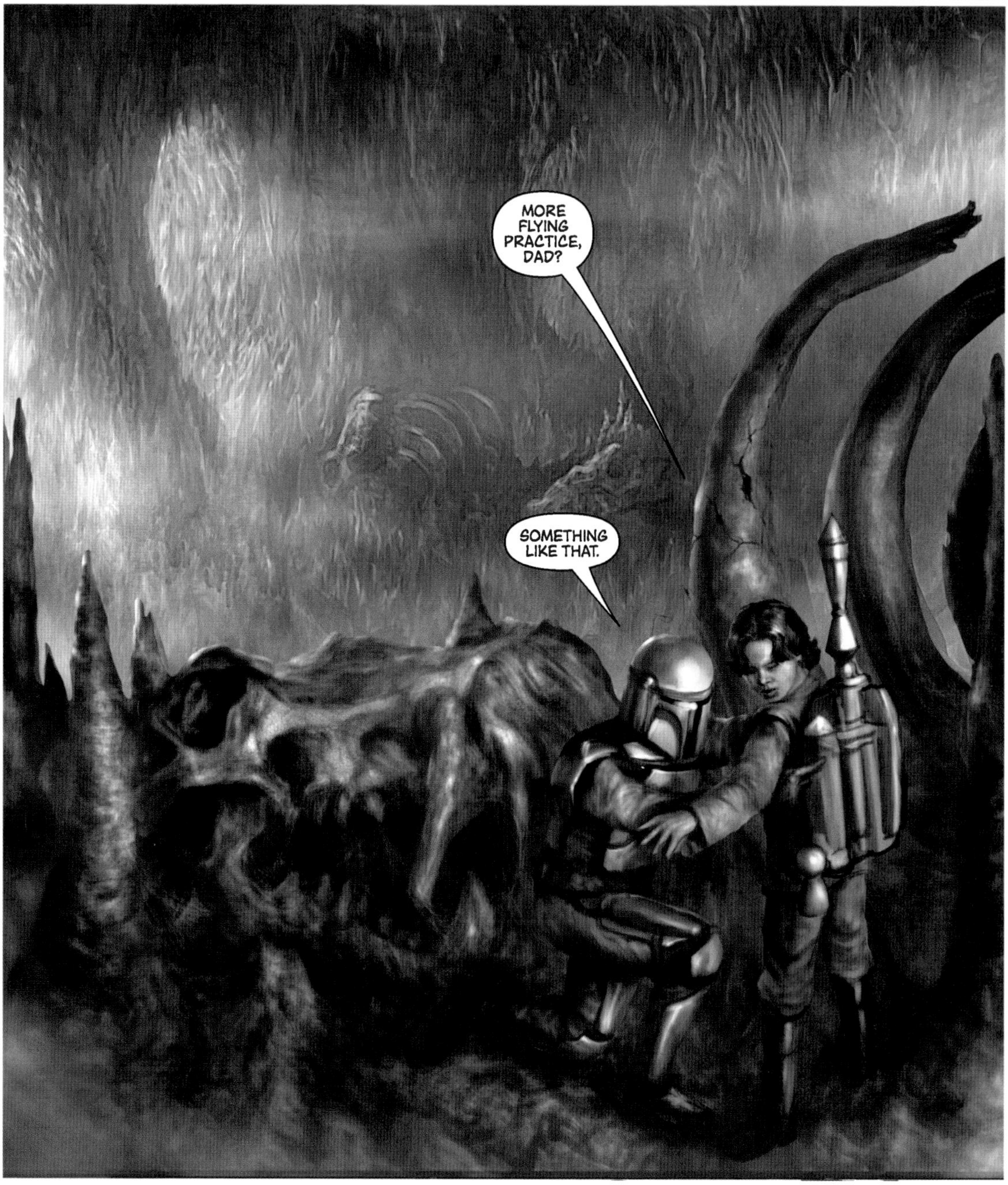
MORE FLYING PRACTICE, DAD?
SOMETHING LIKE THAT.

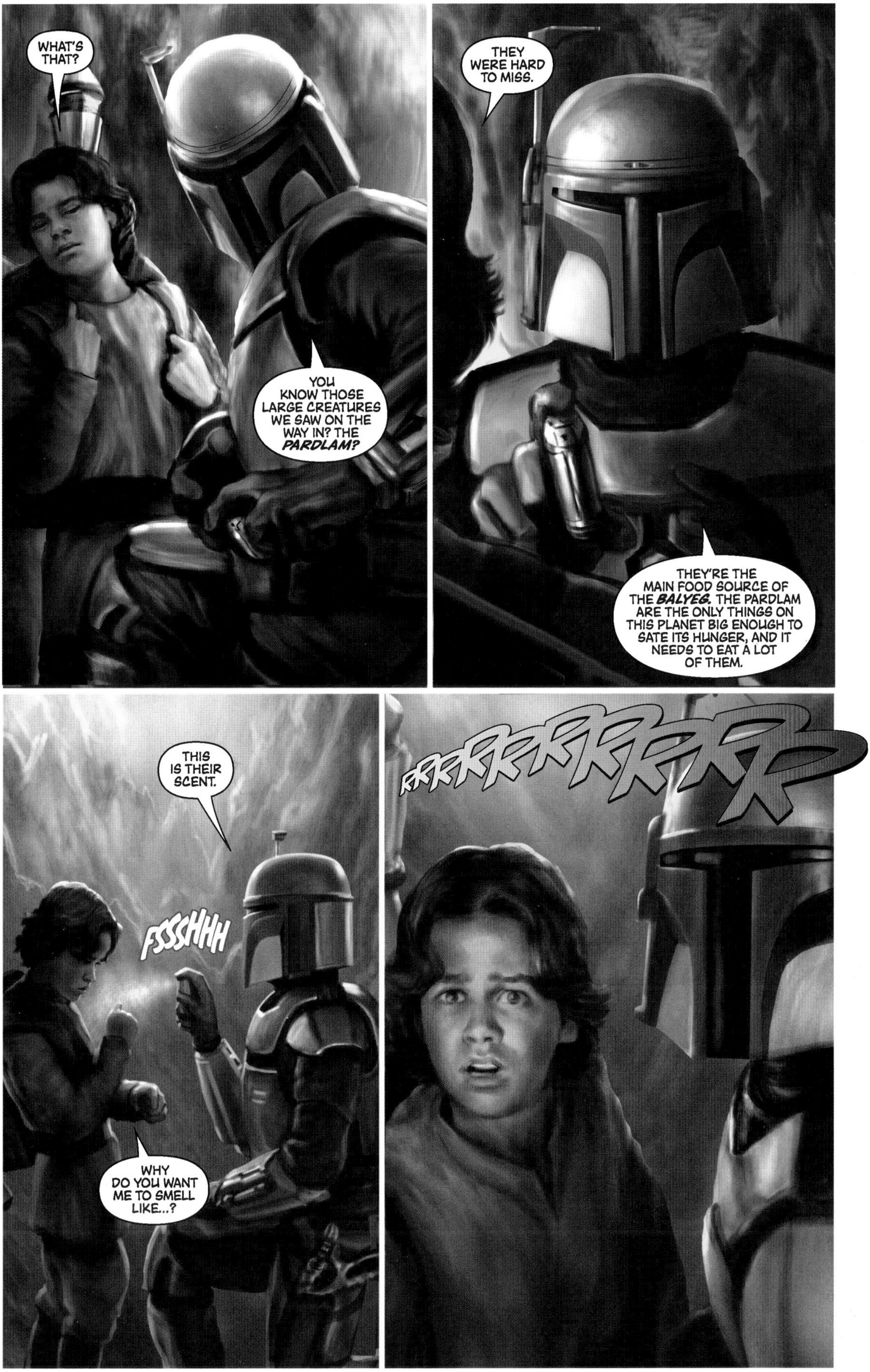
WHAT'S THAT?
YOU KNOW THOSE LARGE CREATURES WE SAW ON THE WAY IN? THE *PARDLAM?*
THEY WERE HARD TO MISS.
THEY'RE THE MAIN FOOD SOURCE OF THE *BALYEG.* THE PARDLAM ARE THE ONLY THINGS ON THIS PLANET BIG ENOUGH TO SATE ITS HUNGER, AND IT NEEDS TO EAT A LOT OF THEM.
THIS IS THEIR SCENT.
FSSSHHH
WHY DO YOU WANT ME TO SMELL LIKE...?
RRRRRRRRRRRR

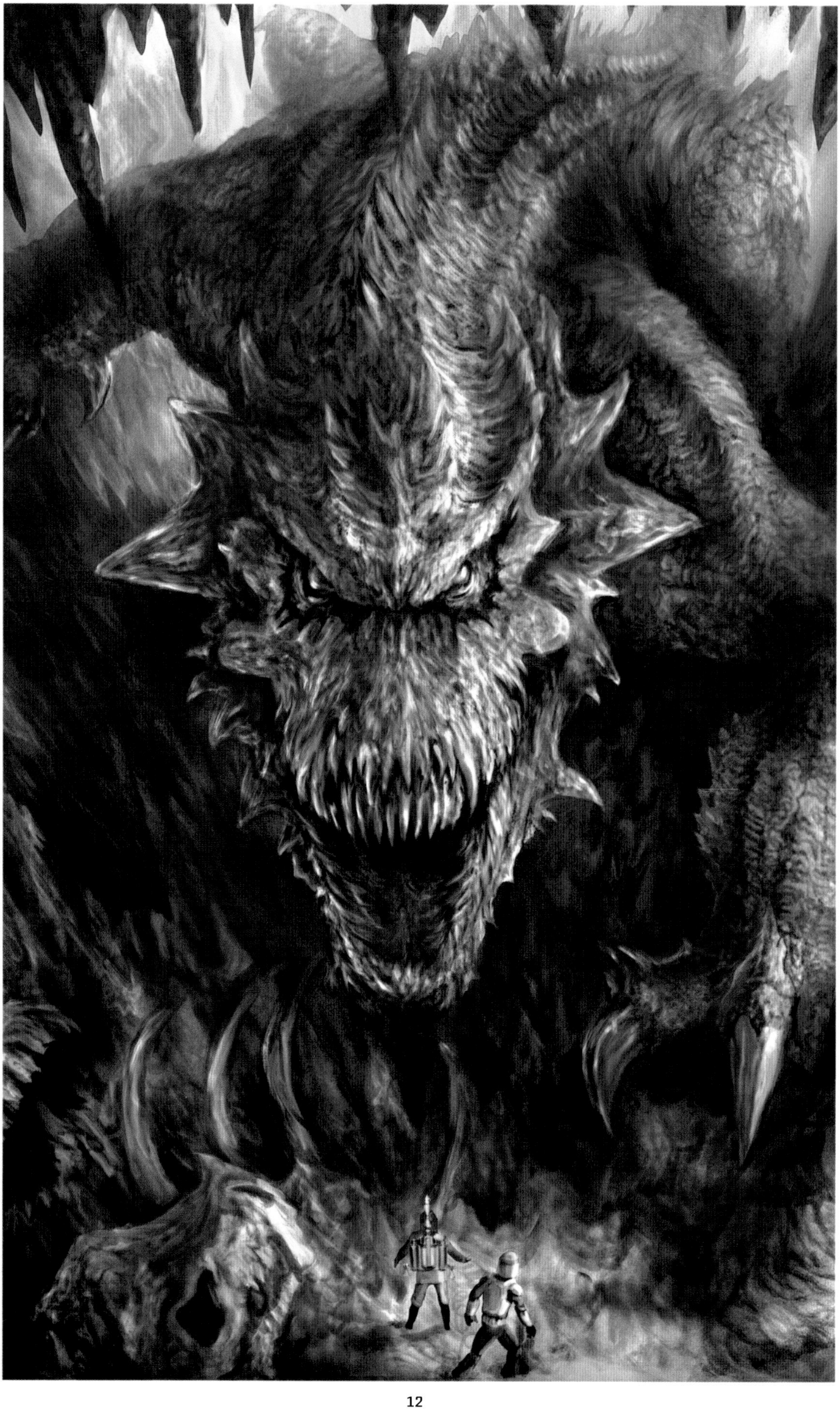

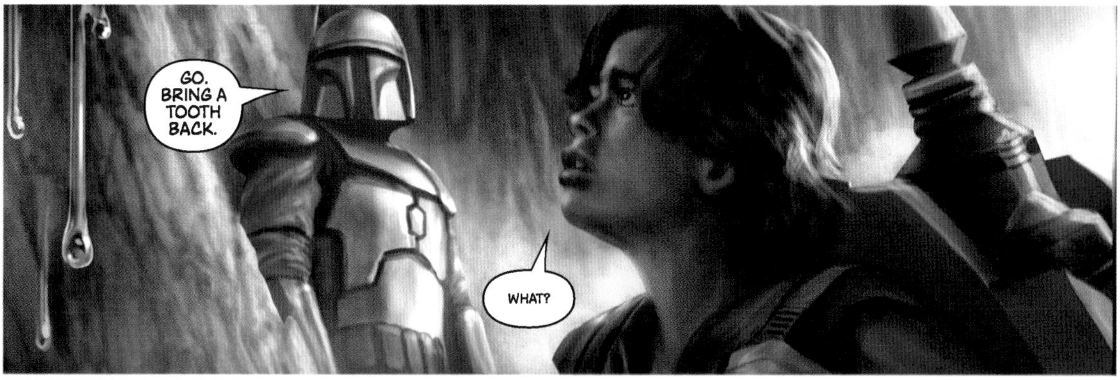
GO. BRING A TOOTH BACK.
WHAT?

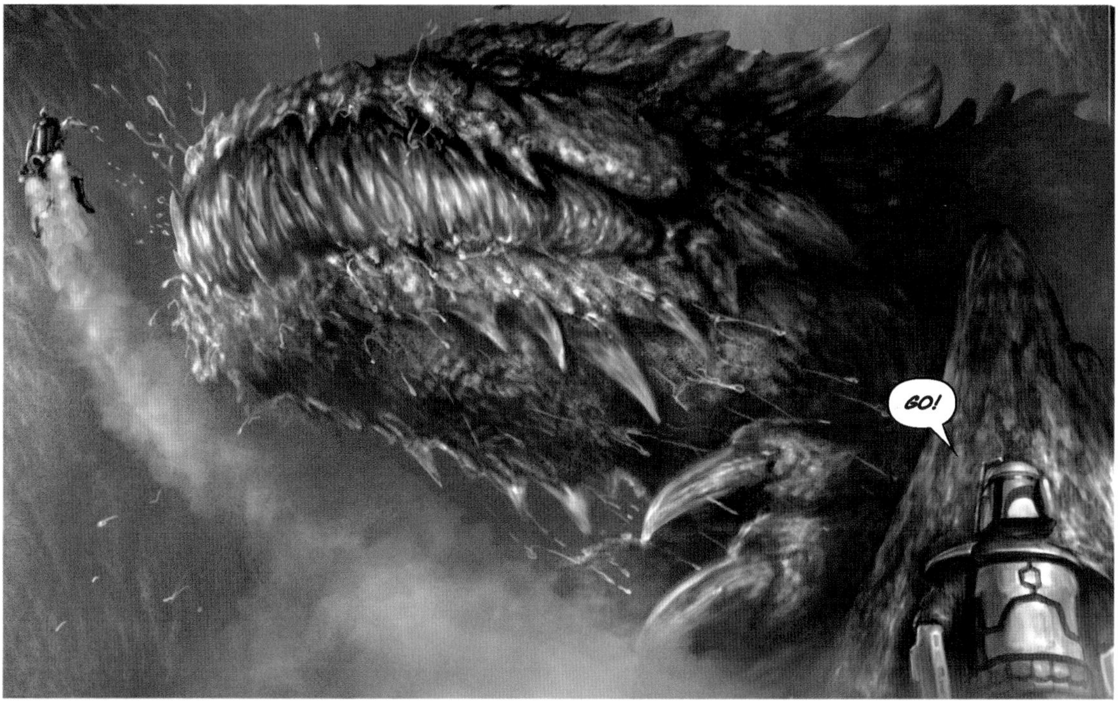
GO!

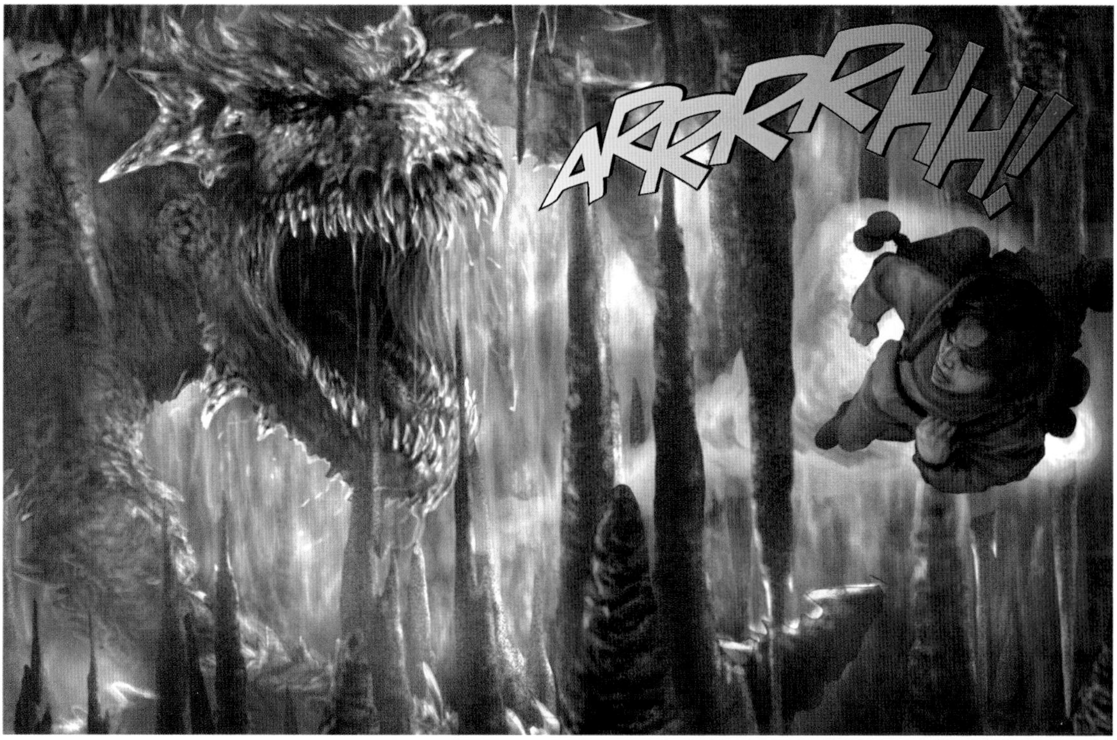
ARRRRRHH!

RRRMMMBLE

RAARGHH!

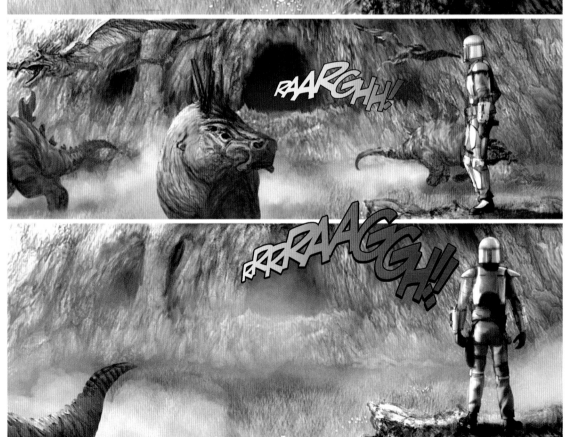

RRRRAAGGH!!

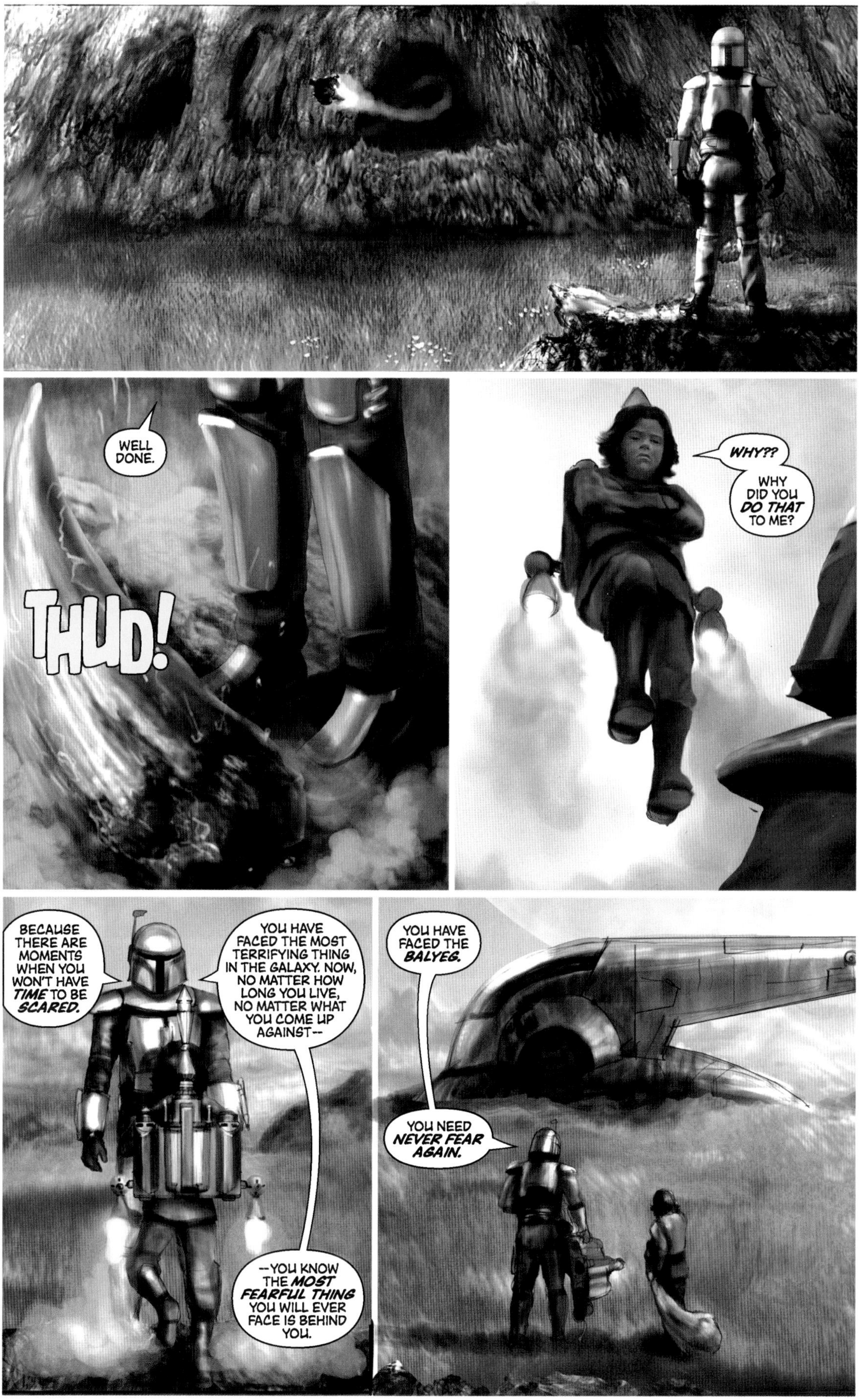
WELL DONE.
THUD!
WHY?? WHY DID YOU DO THAT TO ME?
BECAUSE THERE ARE MOMENTS WHEN YOU WON'T HAVE TIME TO BE SCARED.
YOU HAVE FACED THE MOST TERRIFYING THING IN THE GALAXY. NOW, NO MATTER HOW LONG YOU LIVE, NO MATTER WHAT YOU COME UP AGAINST--
--YOU KNOW THE MOST FEARFUL THING YOU WILL EVER FACE IS BEHIND YOU.
YOU HAVE FACED THE BALYEG.
YOU NEED NEVER FEAR AGAIN.

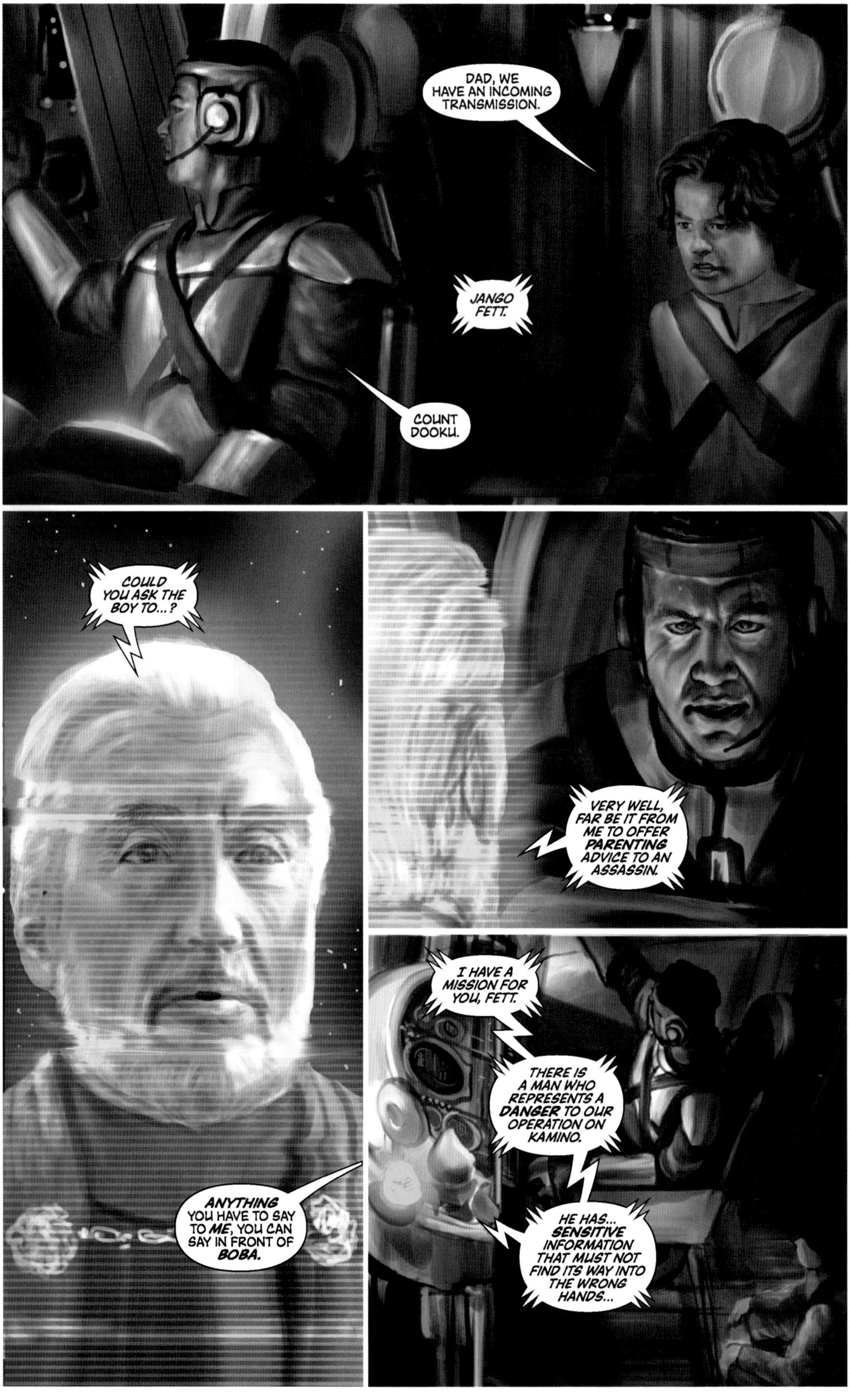
DAD, WE HAVE AN INCOMING TRANSMISSION.
JANGO FETT.
COUNT DOOKU.
COULD YOU ASK THE BOY TO...?
ANYTHING YOU HAVE TO SAY TO ME, YOU CAN SAY IN FRONT OF BOBA.
VERY WELL, FAR BE IT FROM ME TO OFFER PARENTING ADVICE TO AN ASSASSIN.
I HAVE A MISSION FOR YOU, FETT.
THERE IS A MAN WHO REPRESENTS A DANGER TO OUR OPERATION ON KAMINO.
HE HAS... SENSITIVE INFORMATION THAT MUST NOT FIND ITS WAY INTO THE WRONG HANDS...

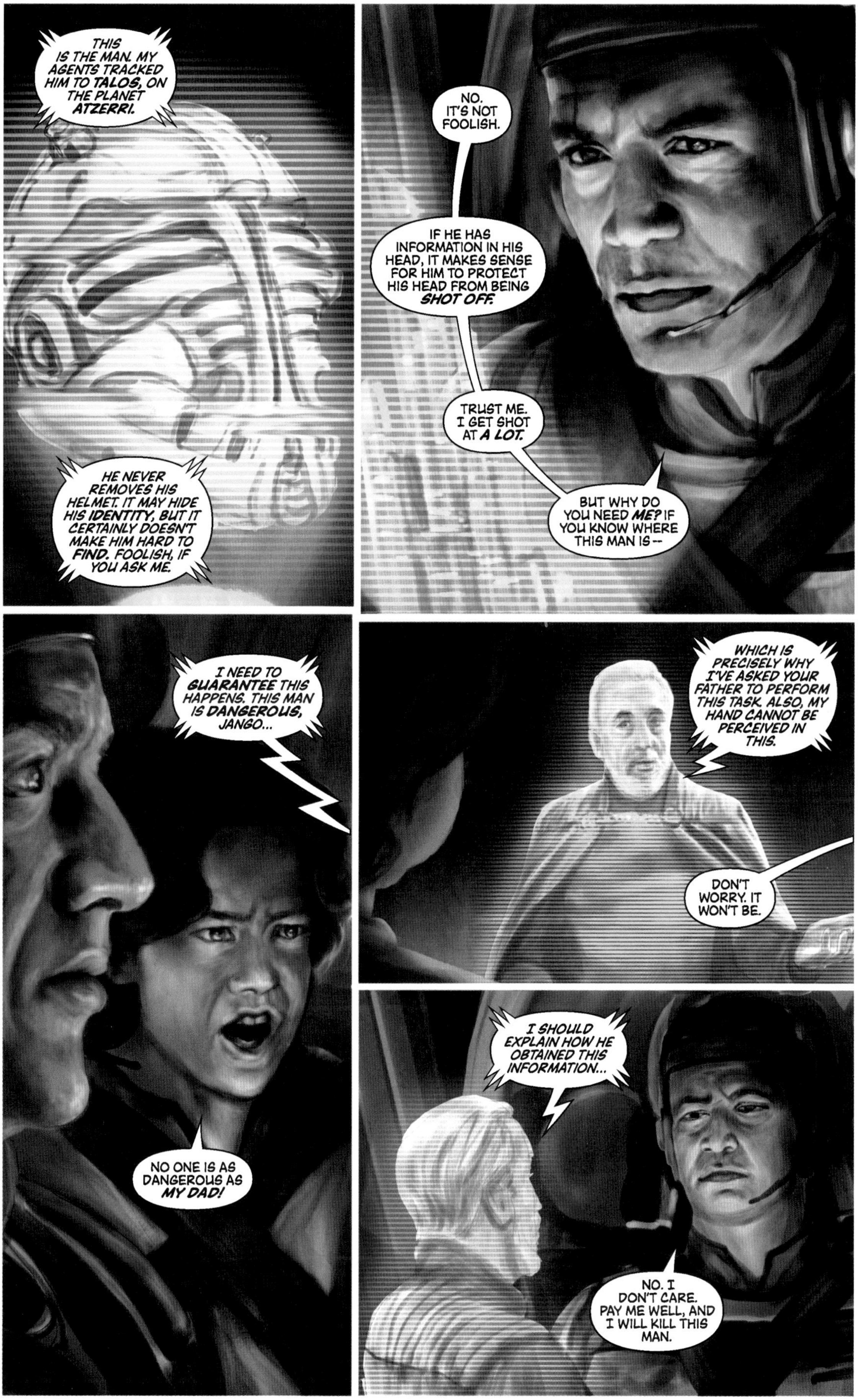
THIS IS THE MAN. MY AGENTS TRACKED HIM TO TALOS, ON THE PLANET ATZERRI.
HE NEVER REMOVES HIS HELMET. IT MAY HIDE HIS IDENTITY, BUT IT CERTAINLY DOESN'T MAKE HIM HARD TO FIND. FOOLISH, IF YOU ASK ME.
NO. IT'S NOT FOOLISH.
IF HE HAS INFORMATION IN HIS HEAD, IT MAKES SENSE FOR HIM TO PROTECT HIS HEAD FROM BEING SHOT OFF.
TRUST ME. I GET SHOT AT A LOT.
BUT WHY DO YOU NEED ME? IF YOU KNOW WHERE THIS MAN IS --
I NEED TO GUARANTEE THIS HAPPENS. THIS MAN IS DANGEROUS, JANGO...
NO ONE IS AS DANGEROUS AS MY DAD!
WHICH IS PRECISELY WHY I'VE ASKED YOUR FATHER TO PERFORM THIS TASK. ALSO, MY HAND CANNOT BE PERCEIVED IN THIS.
DON'T WORRY. IT WON'T BE.
I SHOULD EXPLAIN HOW HE OBTAINED THIS INFORMATION...
NO. I DON'T CARE. PAY ME WELL, AND I WILL KILL THIS MAN.

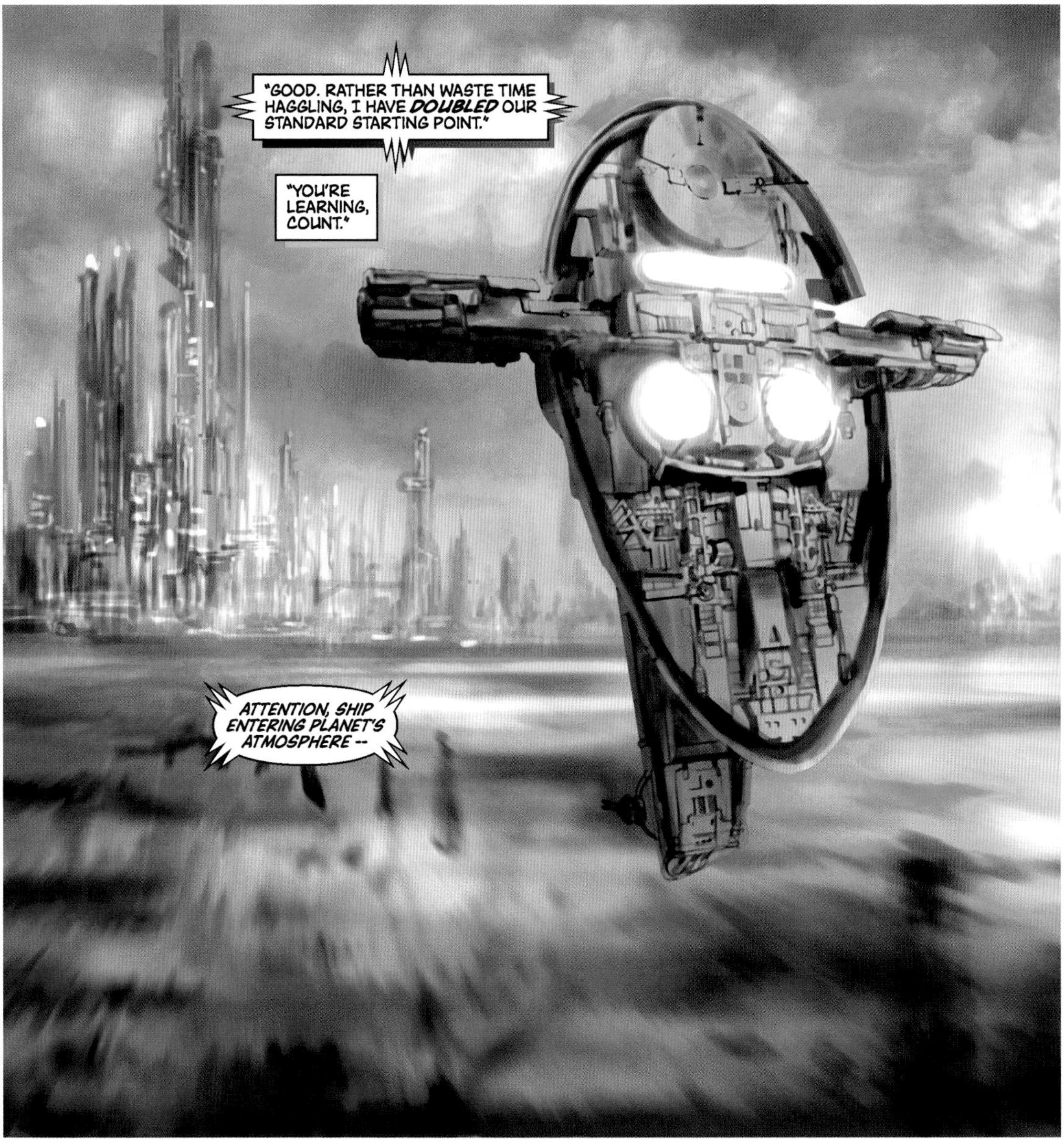
"GOOD. RATHER THAN WASTE TIME HAGGLING, I HAVE DOUBLED OUR STANDARD STARTING POINT."
"YOU'RE LEARNING, COUNT."
ATTENTION, SHIP ENTERING PLANET'S ATMOSPHERE --

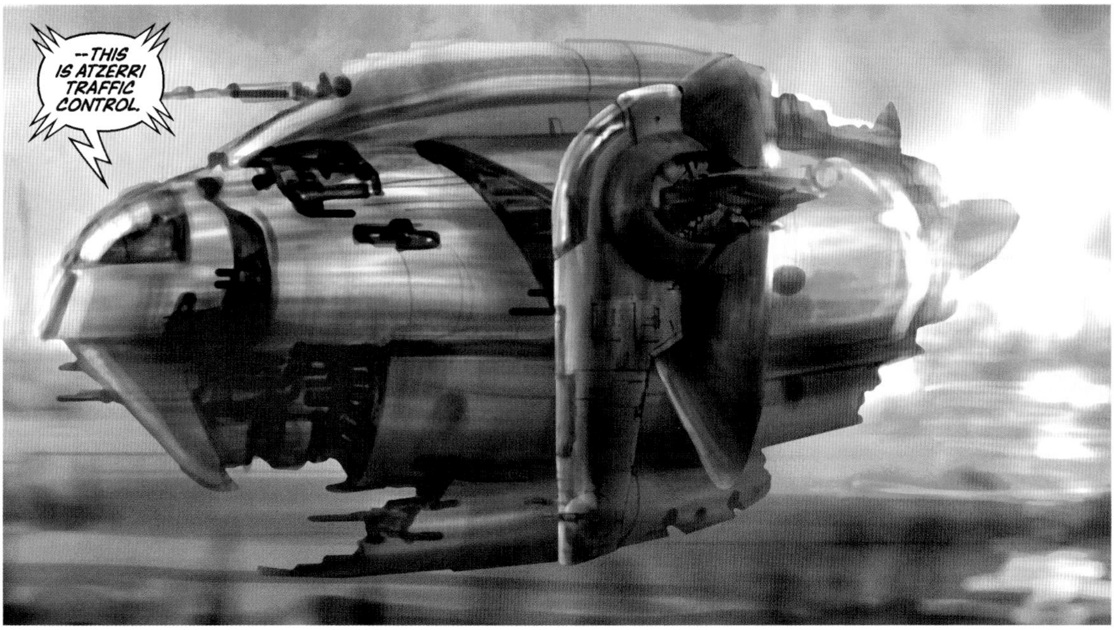
--THIS IS ATZERRI TRAFFIC CONTROL.

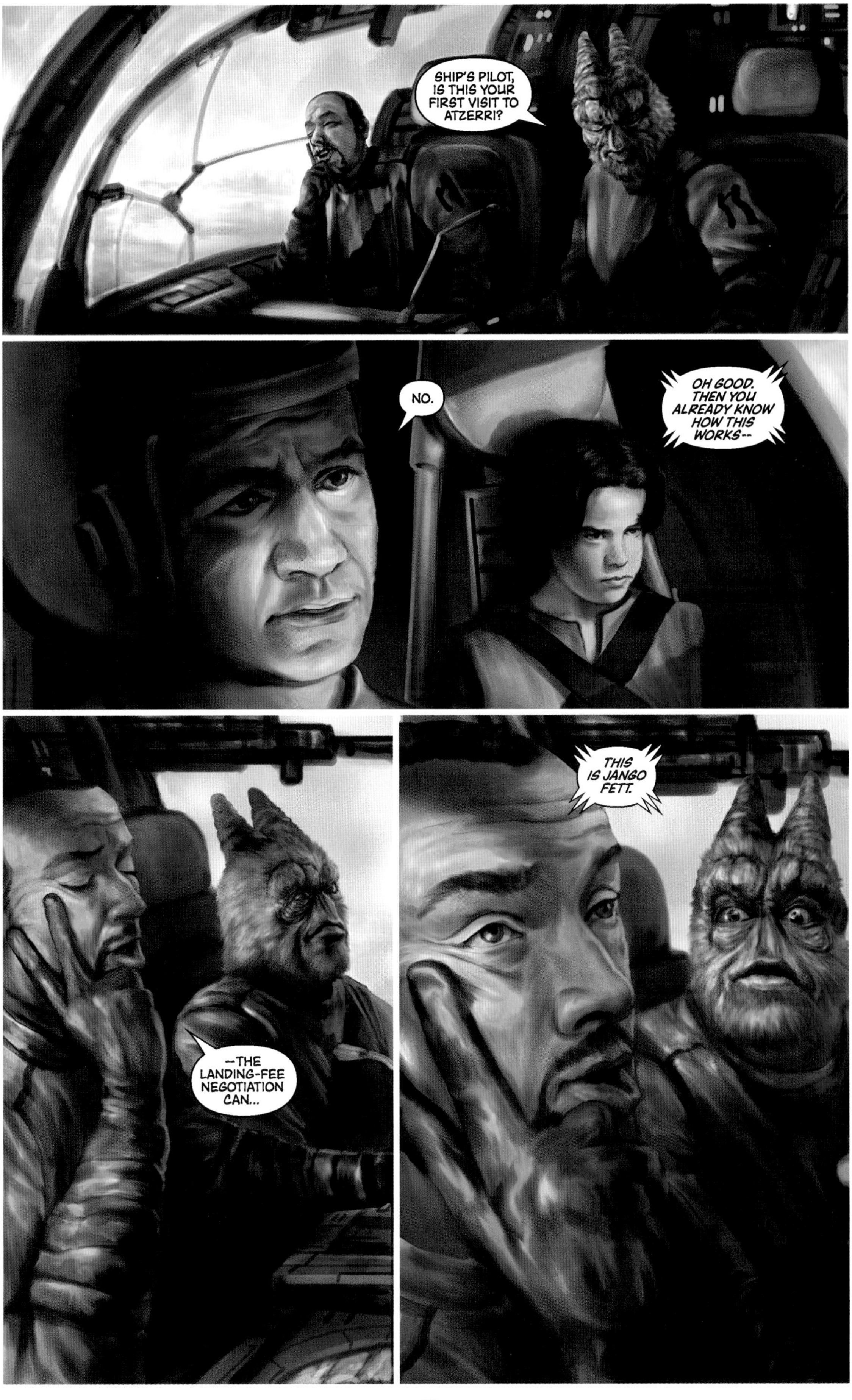
SHIP'S PILOT, IS THIS YOUR FIRST VISIT TO ATZERRI?
NO.
OH GOOD. THEN YOU ALREADY KNOW HOW THIS WORKS--
--THE LANDING-FEE NEGOTIATION CAN...
THIS IS JANGO FETT.

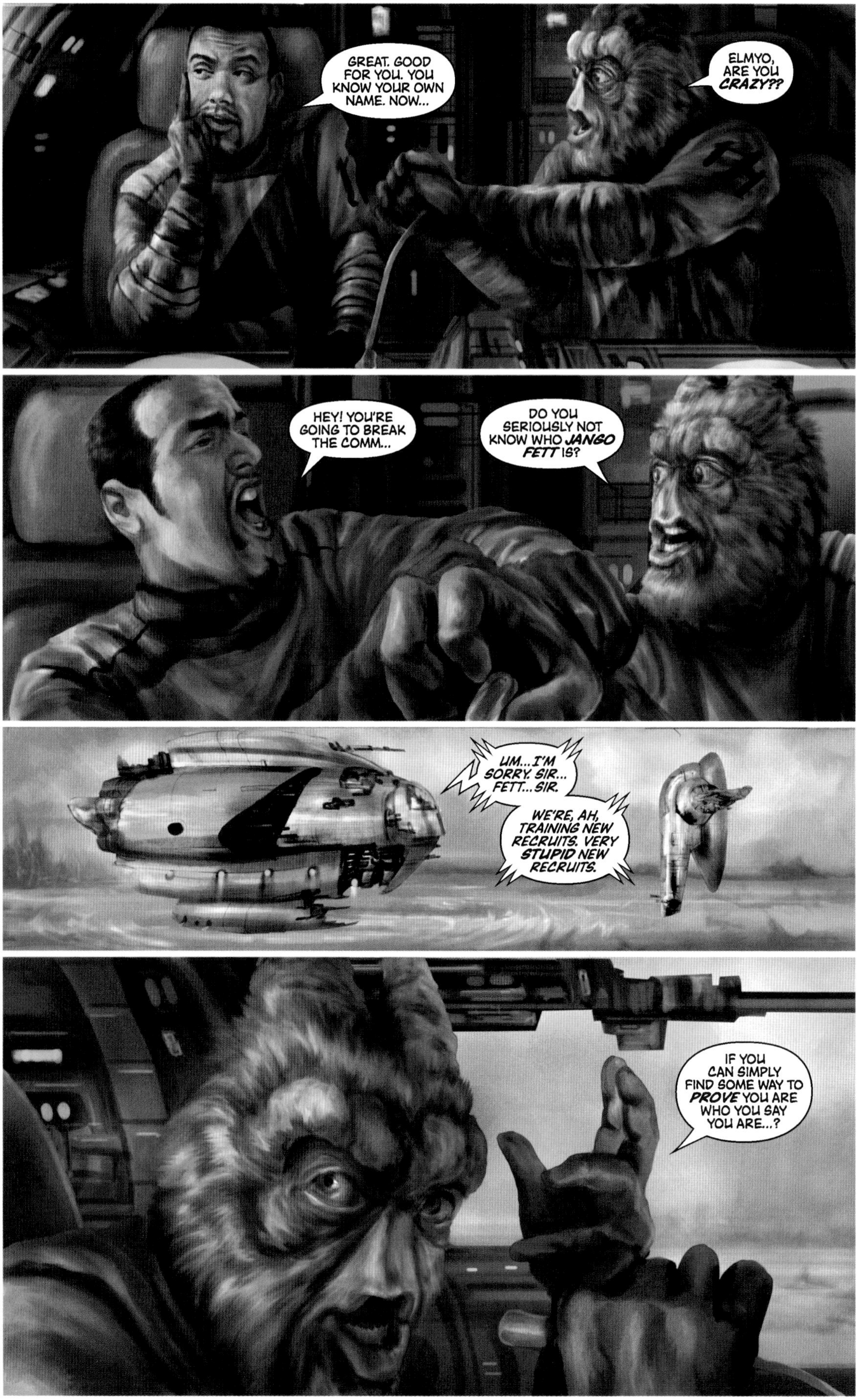
GREAT. GOOD FOR YOU. YOU KNOW YOUR OWN NAME. NOW...
ELMYO, ARE YOU *CRAZY??*
HEY! YOU'RE GOING TO BREAK THE COMM...
DO YOU SERIOUSLY NOT KNOW WHO *JANGO FETT* IS?
UM...I'M SORRY. SIR... FETT...SIR.
WE'RE, AH, TRAINING NEW RECRUITS. VERY *STUPID* NEW RECRUITS.
IF YOU CAN SIMPLY FIND SOME WAY TO *PROVE* YOU ARE WHO YOU SAY YOU ARE...?

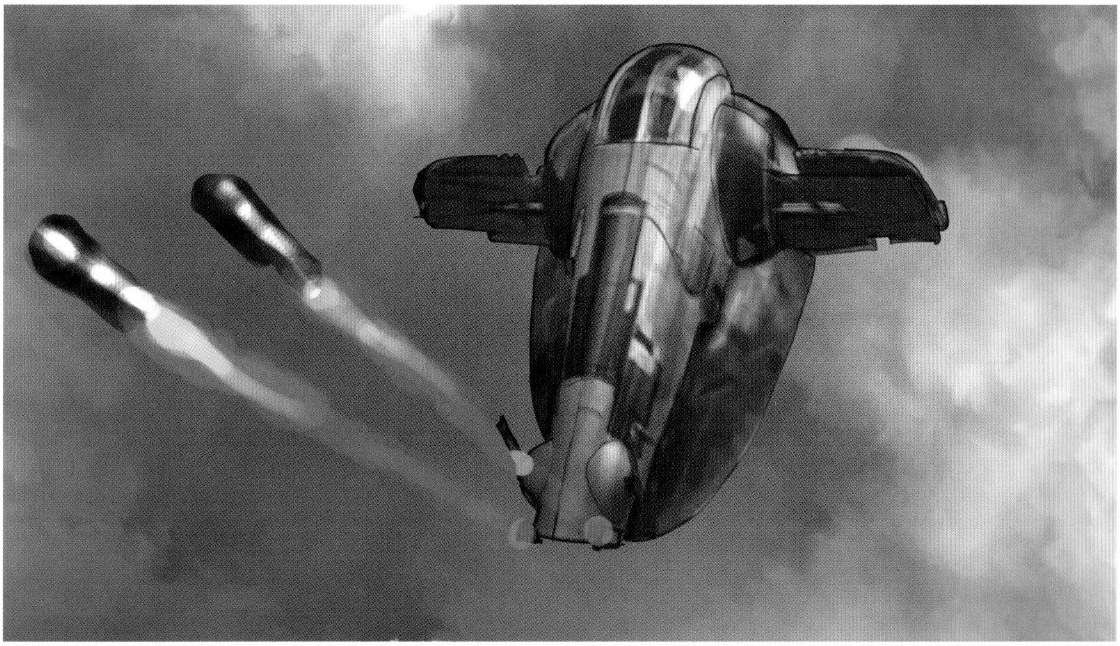

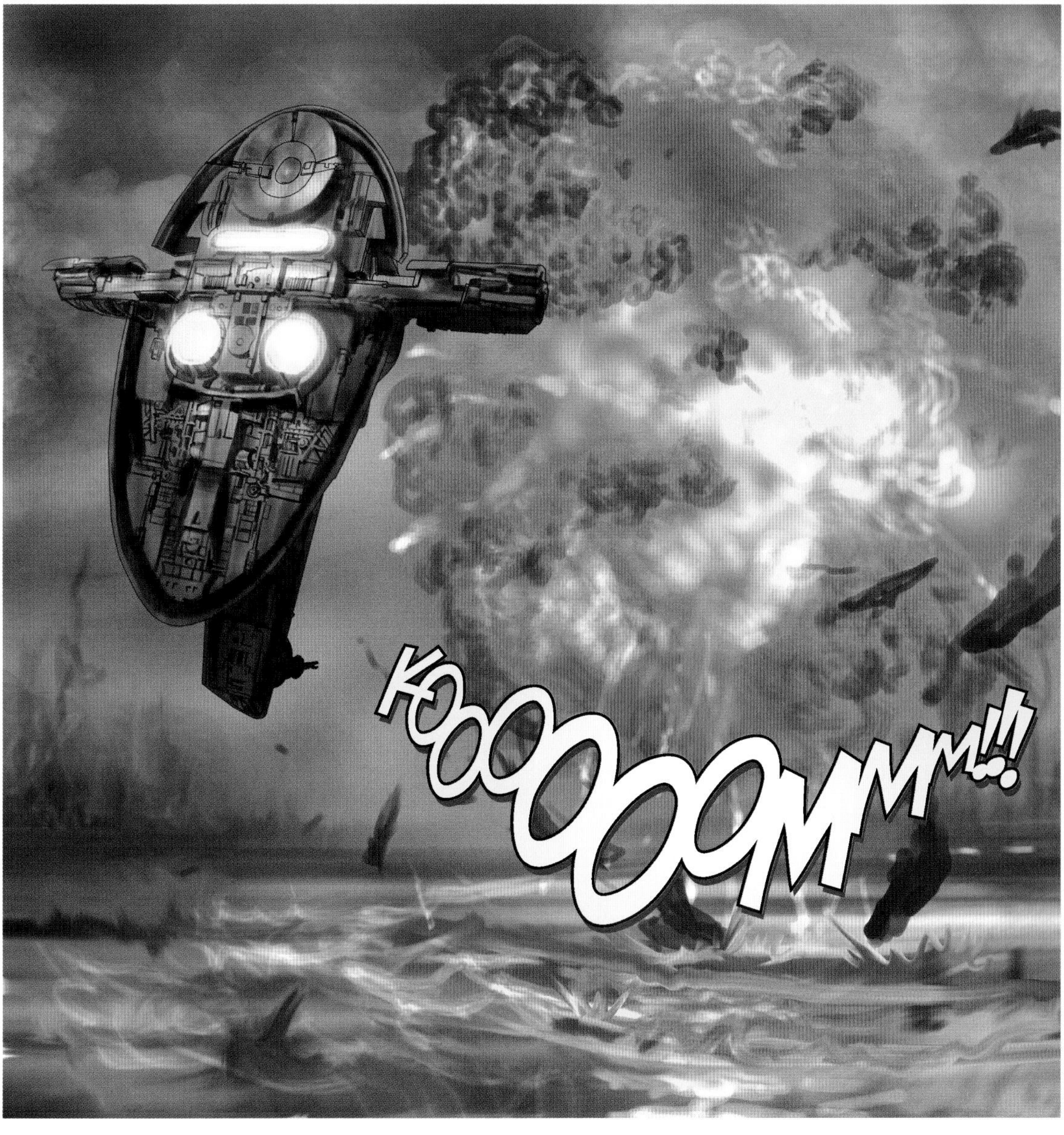
KOOOOOOMMMM!!!

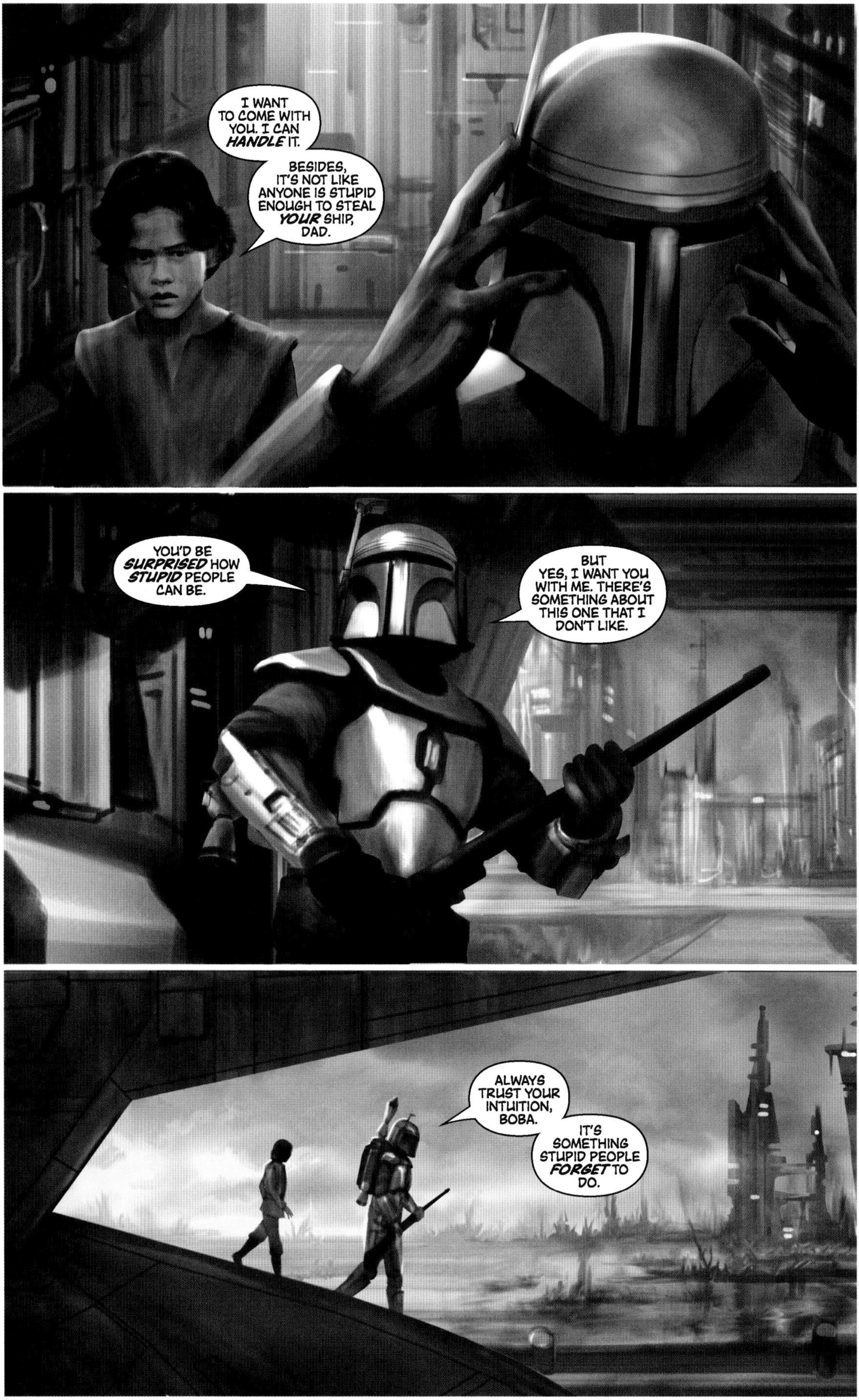
I WANT TO COME WITH YOU. I CAN HANDLE IT.
BESIDES, IT'S NOT LIKE ANYONE IS STUPID ENOUGH TO STEAL YOUR SHIP, DAD.
YOU'D BE SURPRISED HOW STUPID PEOPLE CAN BE.
BUT YES, I WANT YOU WITH ME. THERE'S SOMETHING ABOUT THIS ONE THAT I DON'T LIKE.
ALWAYS TRUST YOUR INTUITION, BOBA.
IT'S SOMETHING STUPID PEOPLE FORGET TO DO.

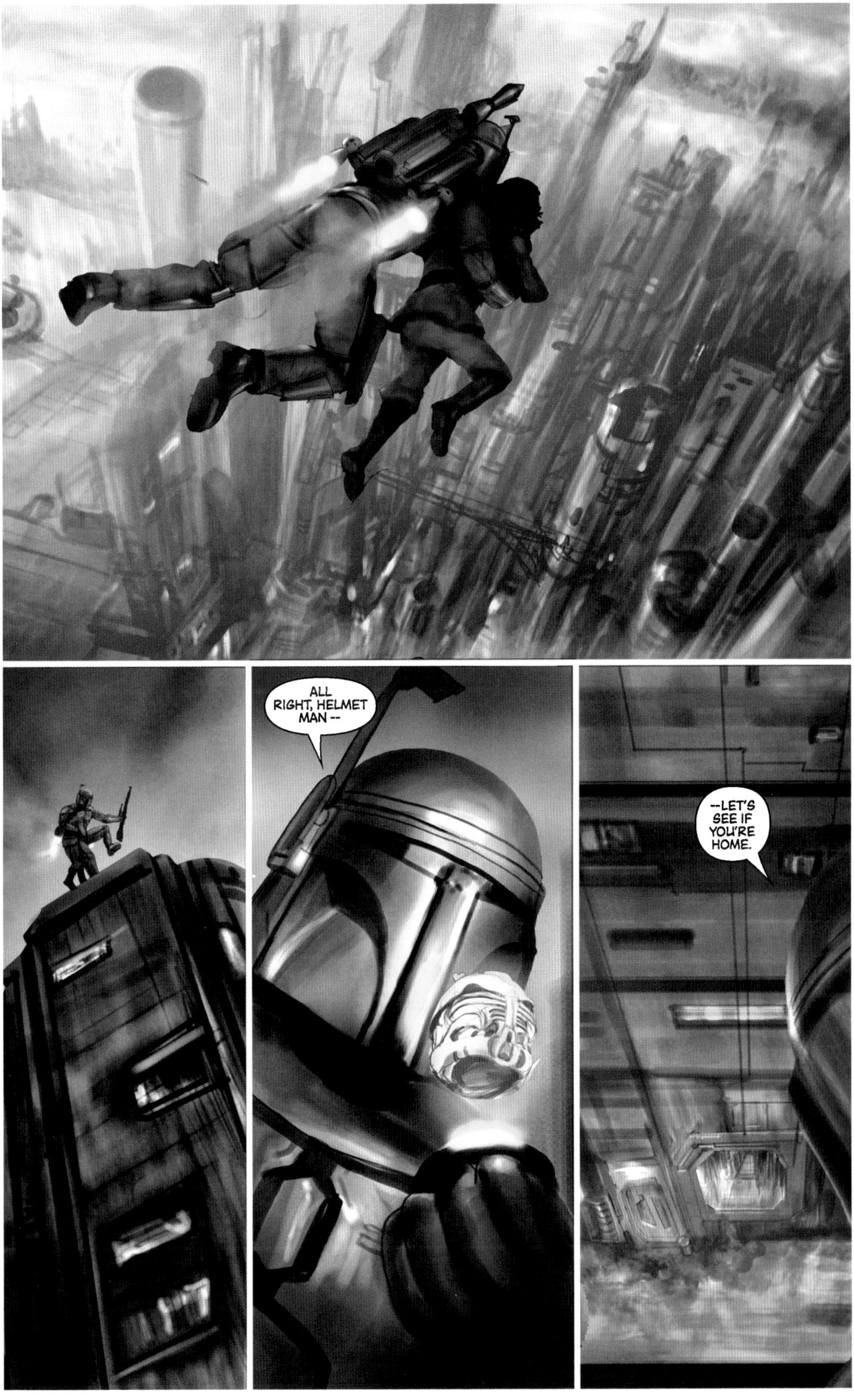
ALL RIGHT, HELMET MAN --
--LET'S SEE IF YOU'RE HOME.

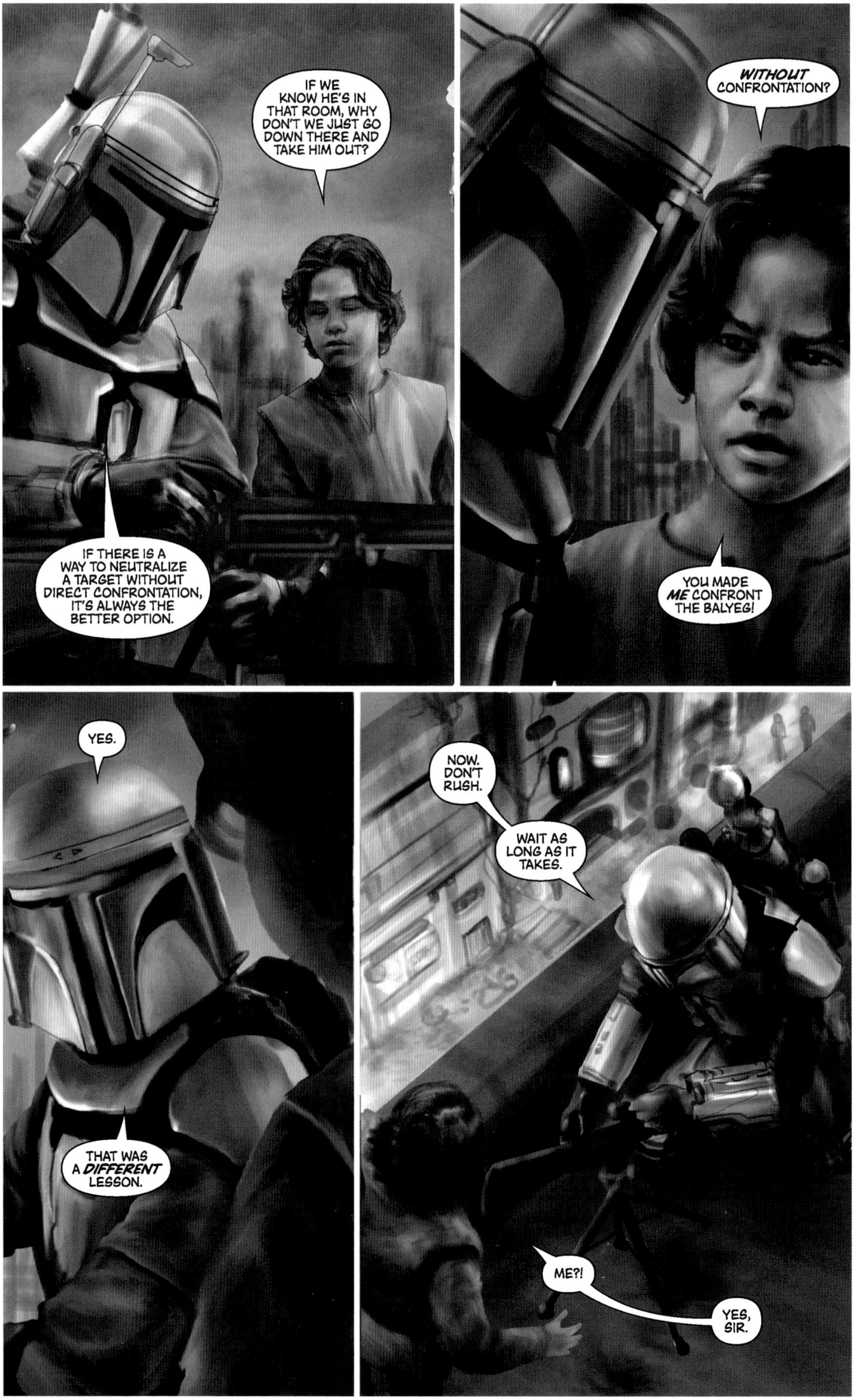
IF WE KNOW HE'S IN THAT ROOM, WHY DON'T WE JUST GO DOWN THERE AND TAKE HIM OUT?
IF THERE IS A WAY TO NEUTRALIZE A TARGET WITHOUT DIRECT CONFRONTATION, IT'S ALWAYS THE BETTER OPTION.
WITHOUT CONFRONTATION?
YOU MADE ME CONFRONT THE BALYEG!
YES.
THAT WAS A DIFFERENT LESSON.
NOW. DON'T RUSH.
WAIT AS LONG AS IT TAKES.
ME?!
YES, SIR.

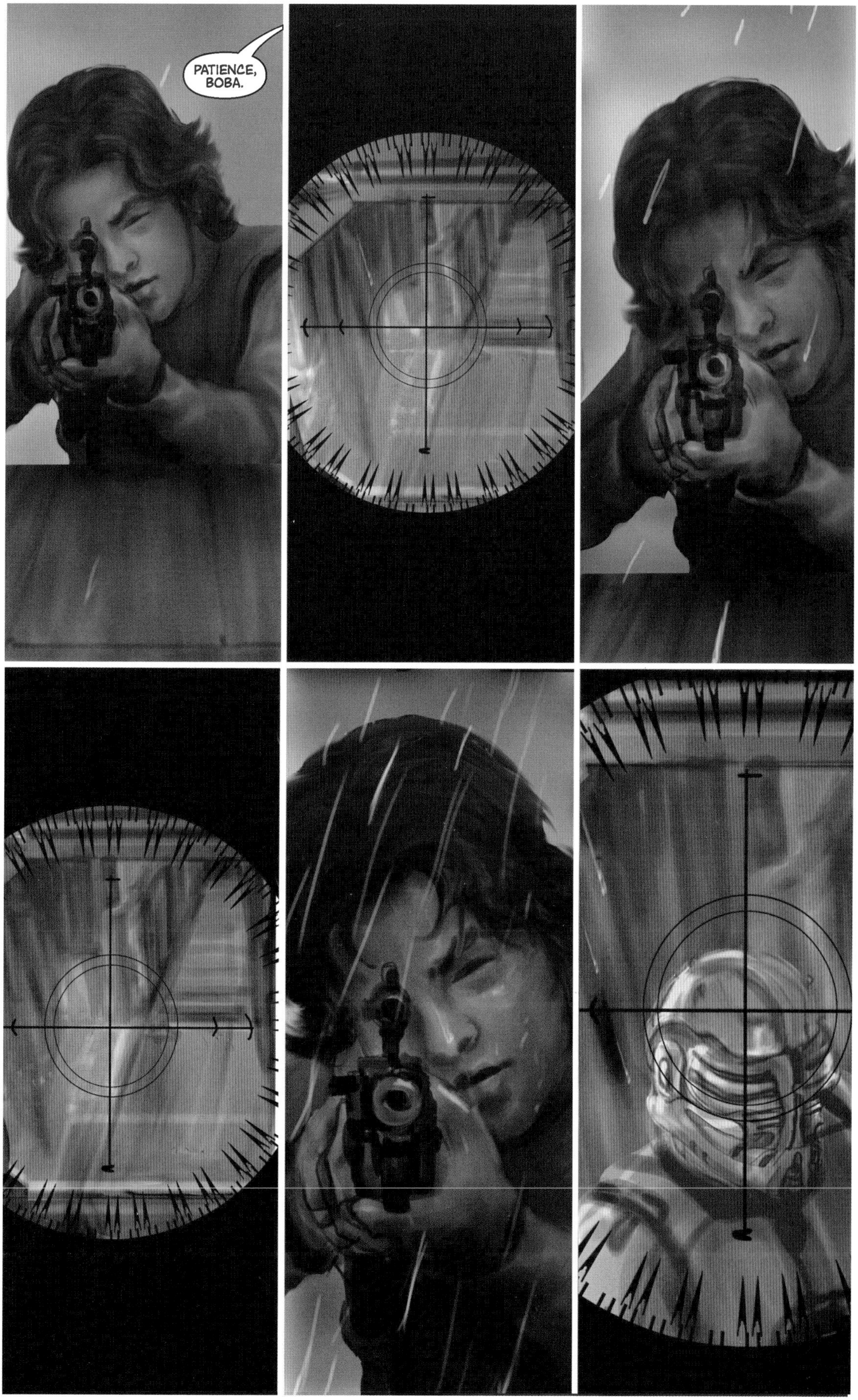
PATIENCE, BOBA.

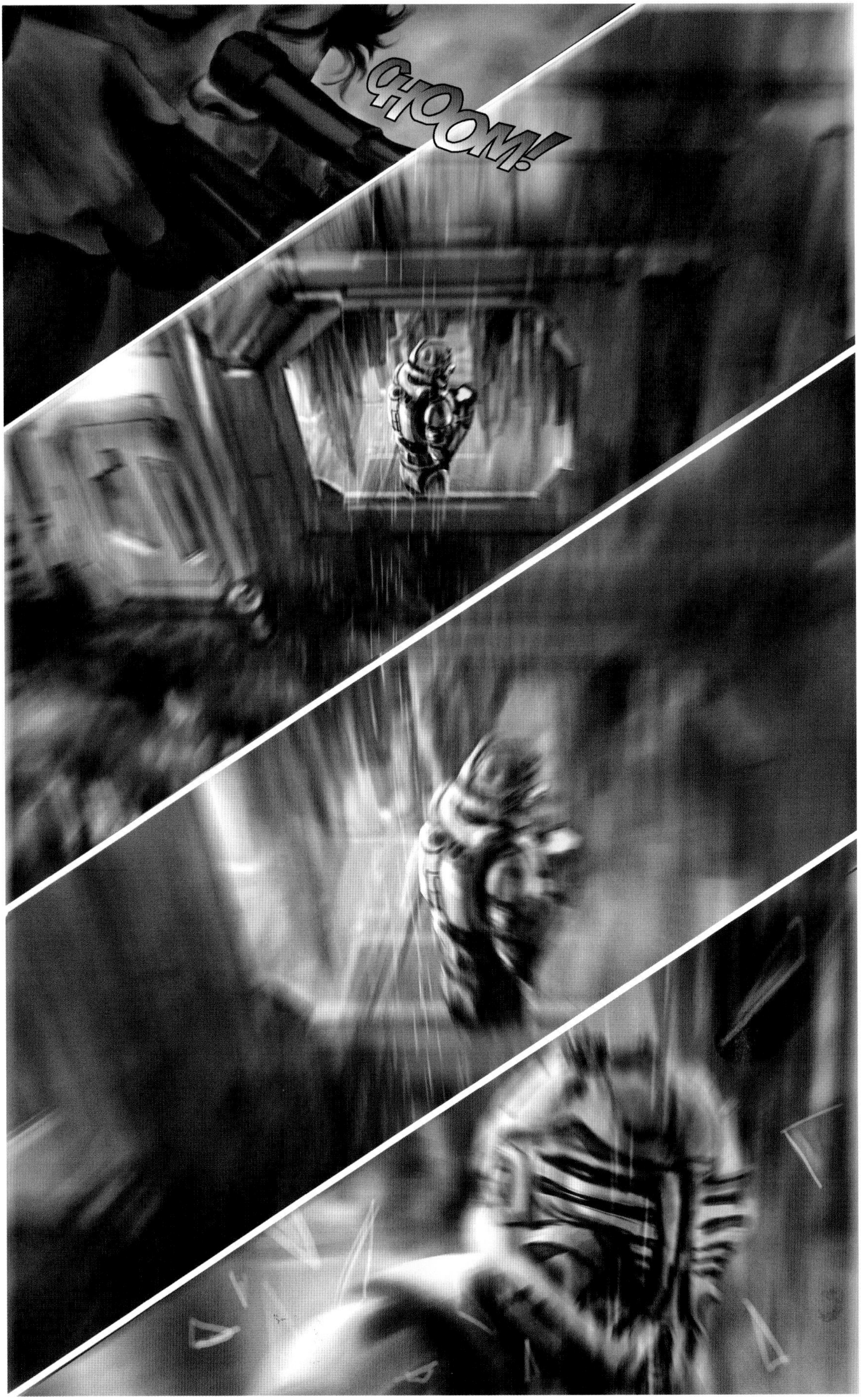
CHOOOM!

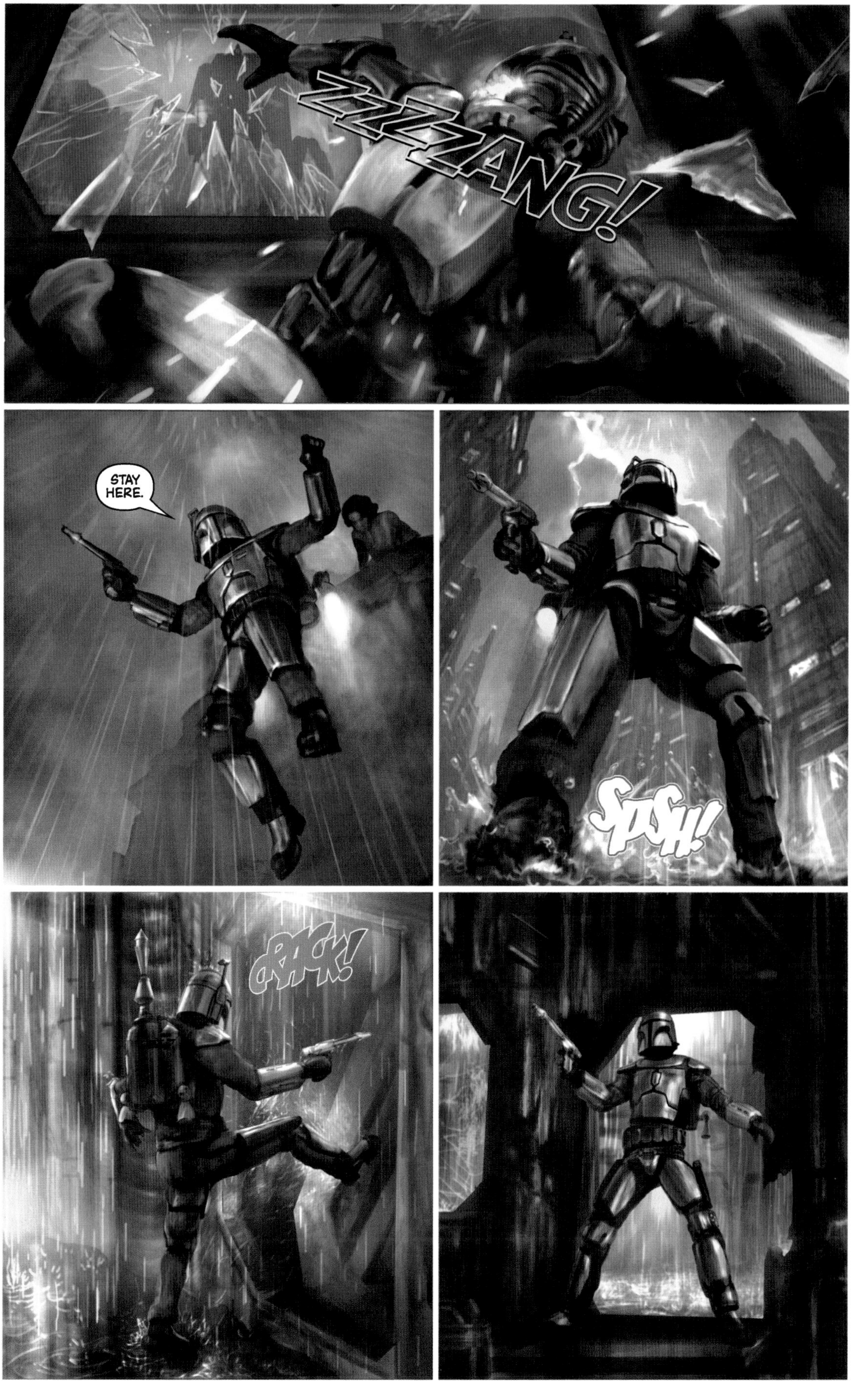
ZZZZANG!
STAY HERE.
SPLSH!
CRACK!

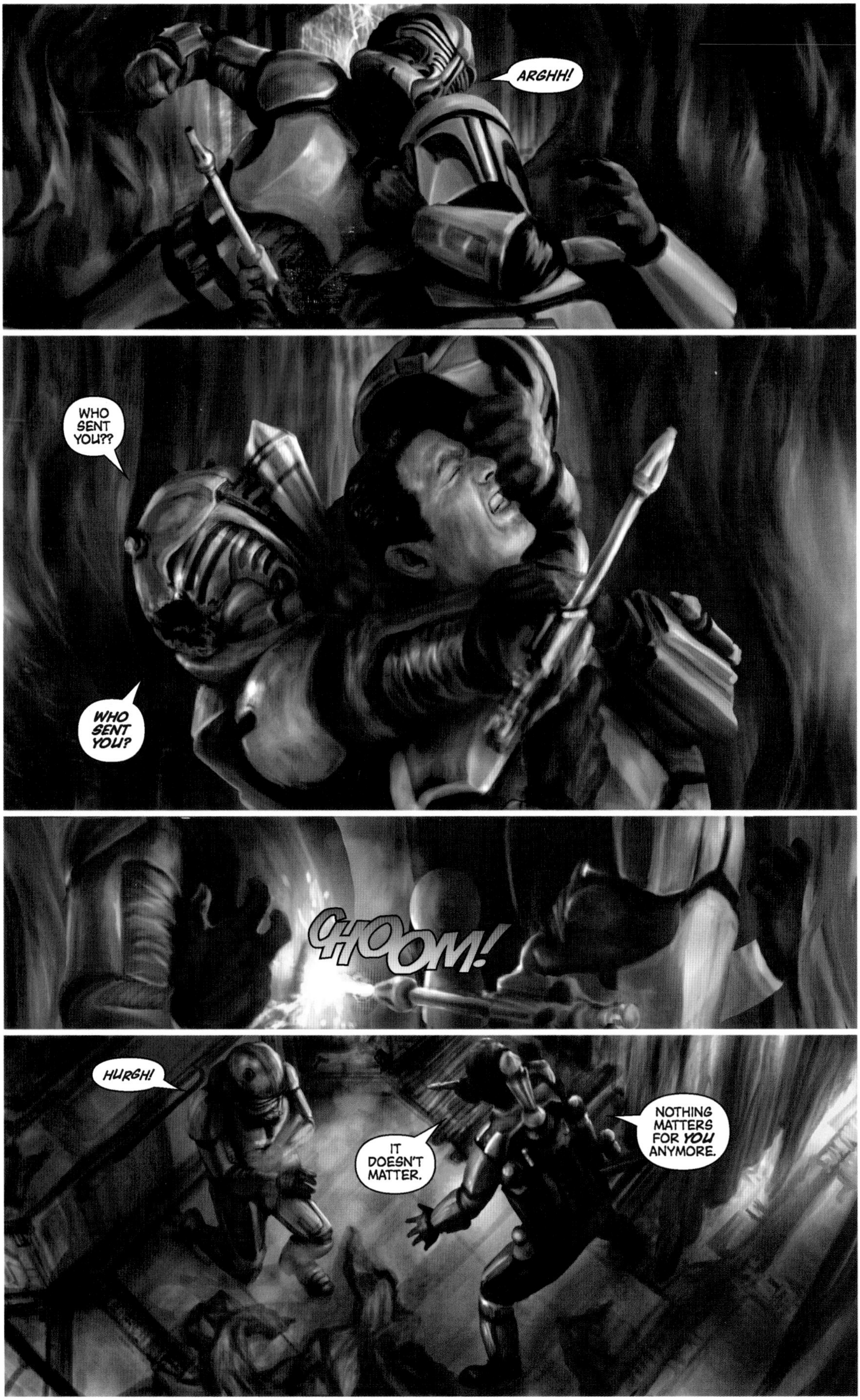
ARGHH!
WHO SENT YOU??
WHO SENT YOU?
CHOOM!
HURGH!
IT DOESN'T MATTER.
NOTHING MATTERS FOR YOU ANYMORE.

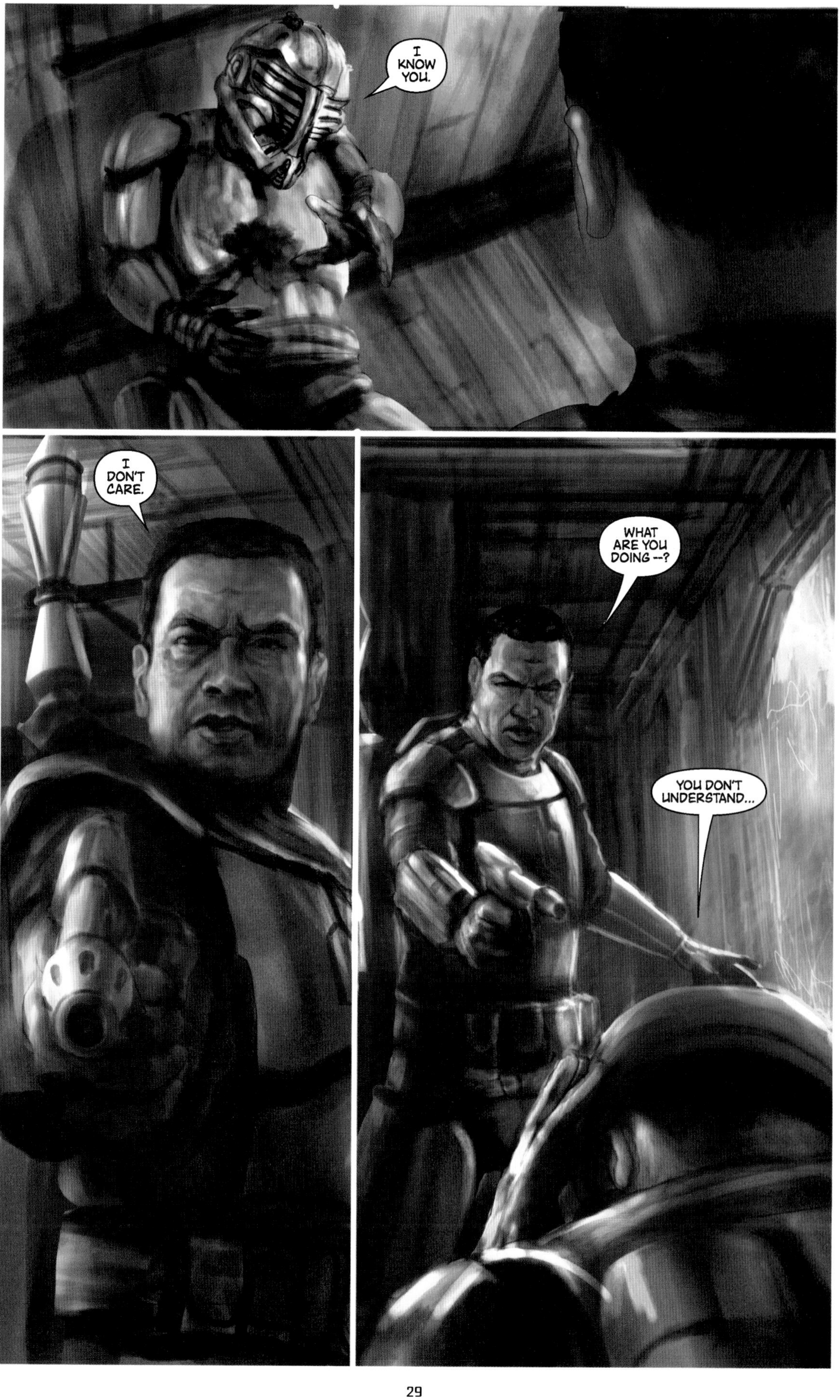
I KNOW YOU.
I DON'T CARE.
WHAT ARE YOU DOING --?
YOU DON'T UNDERSTAND...

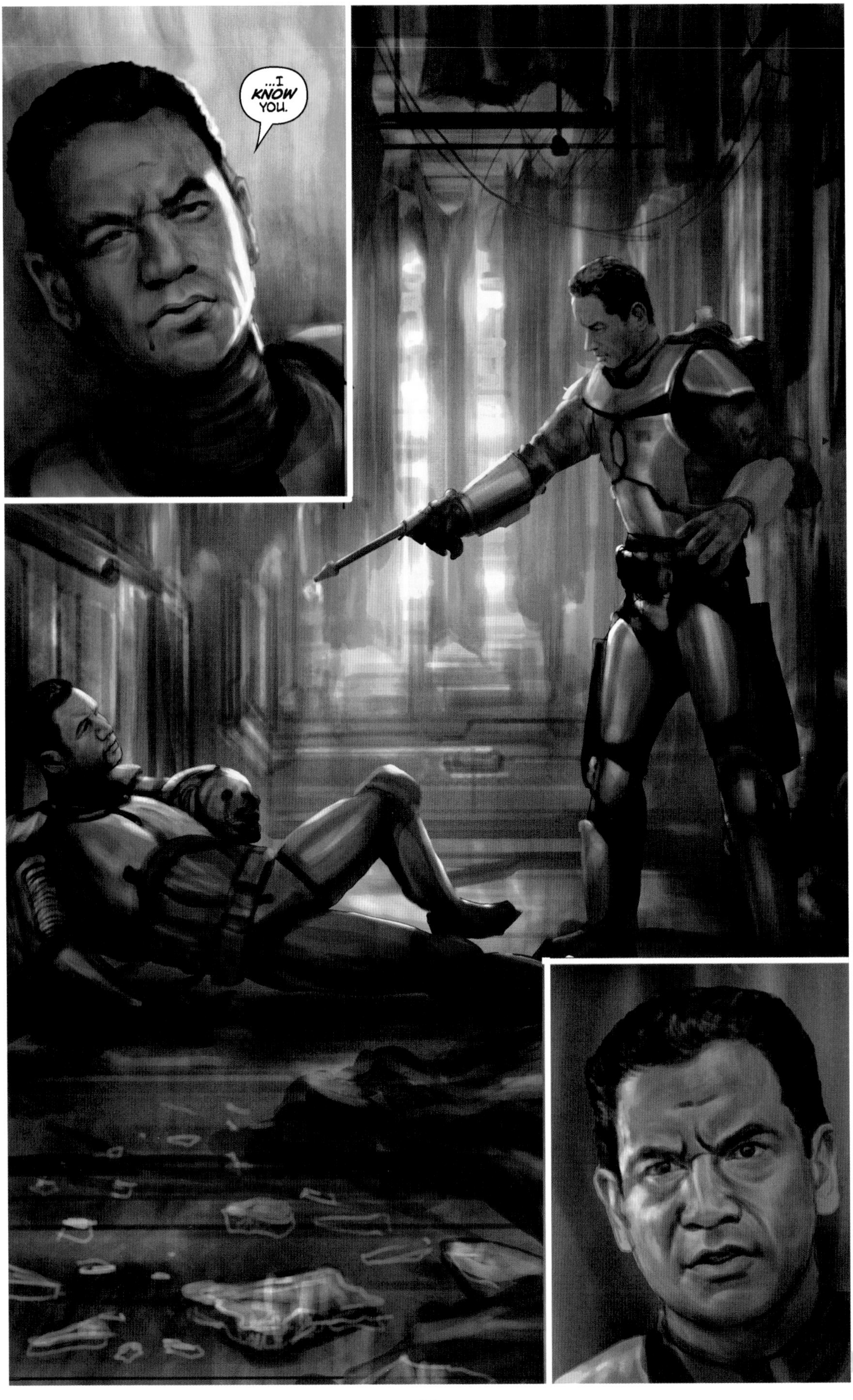
...I KNOW YOU.

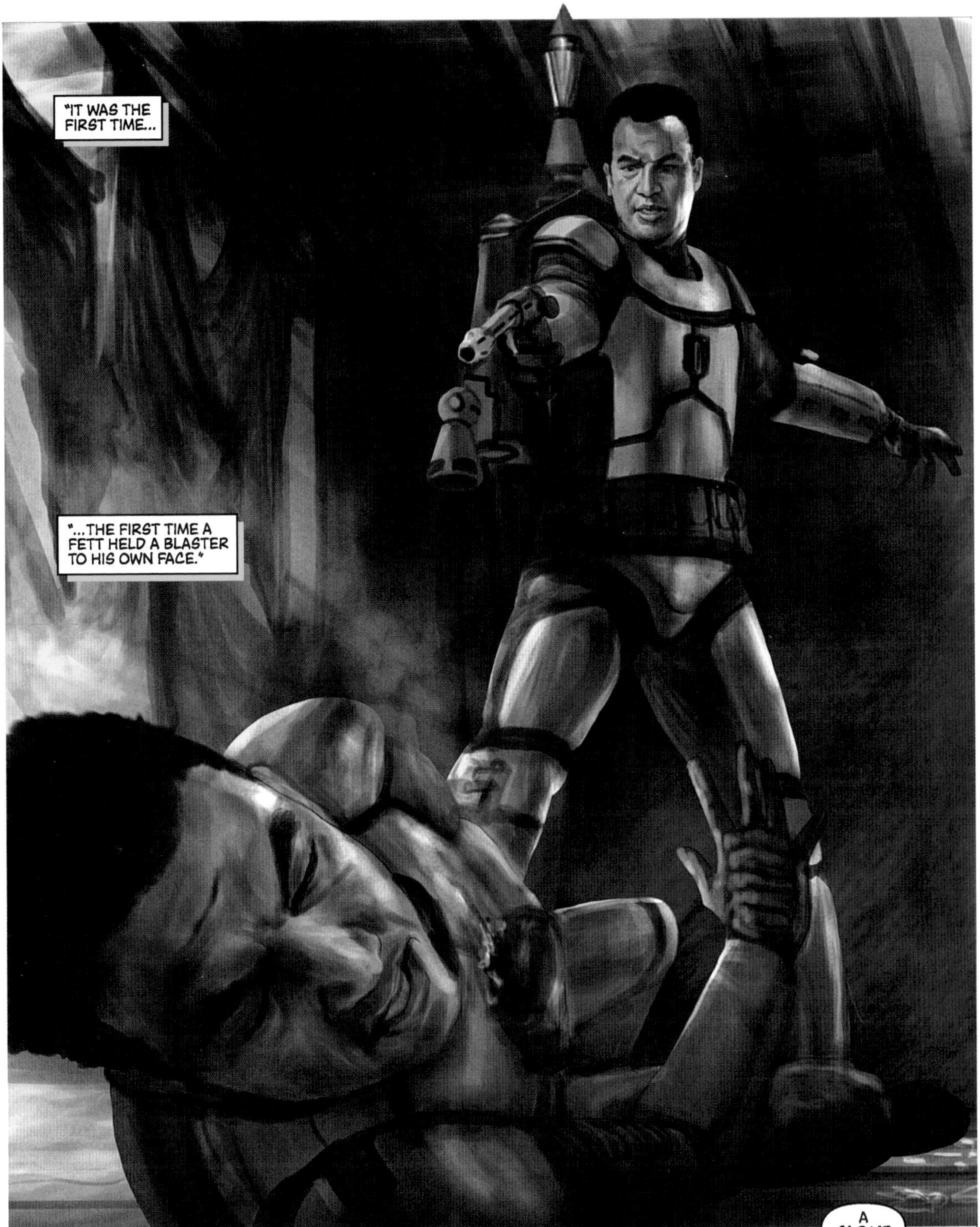
"IT WAS THE FIRST TIME...
"...THE FIRST TIME A FETT HELD A BLASTER TO HIS OWN FACE."

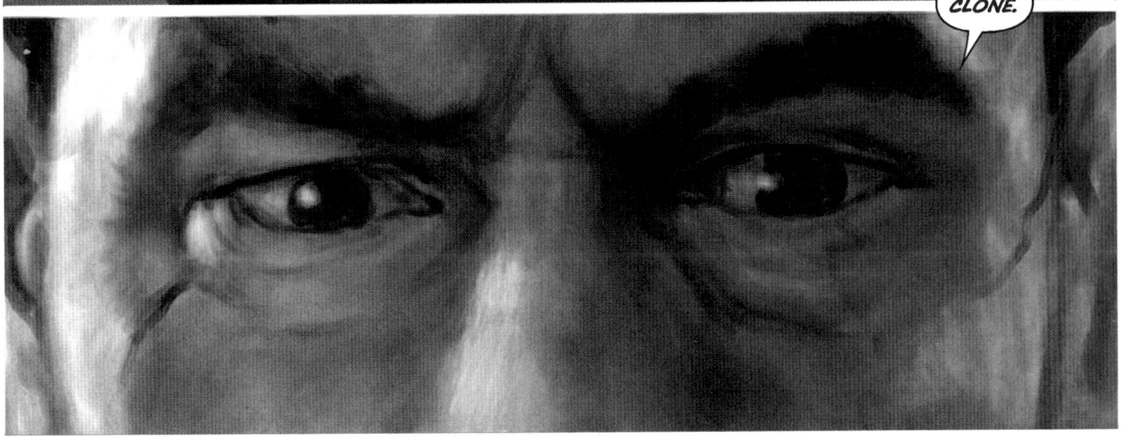
A CLONE.

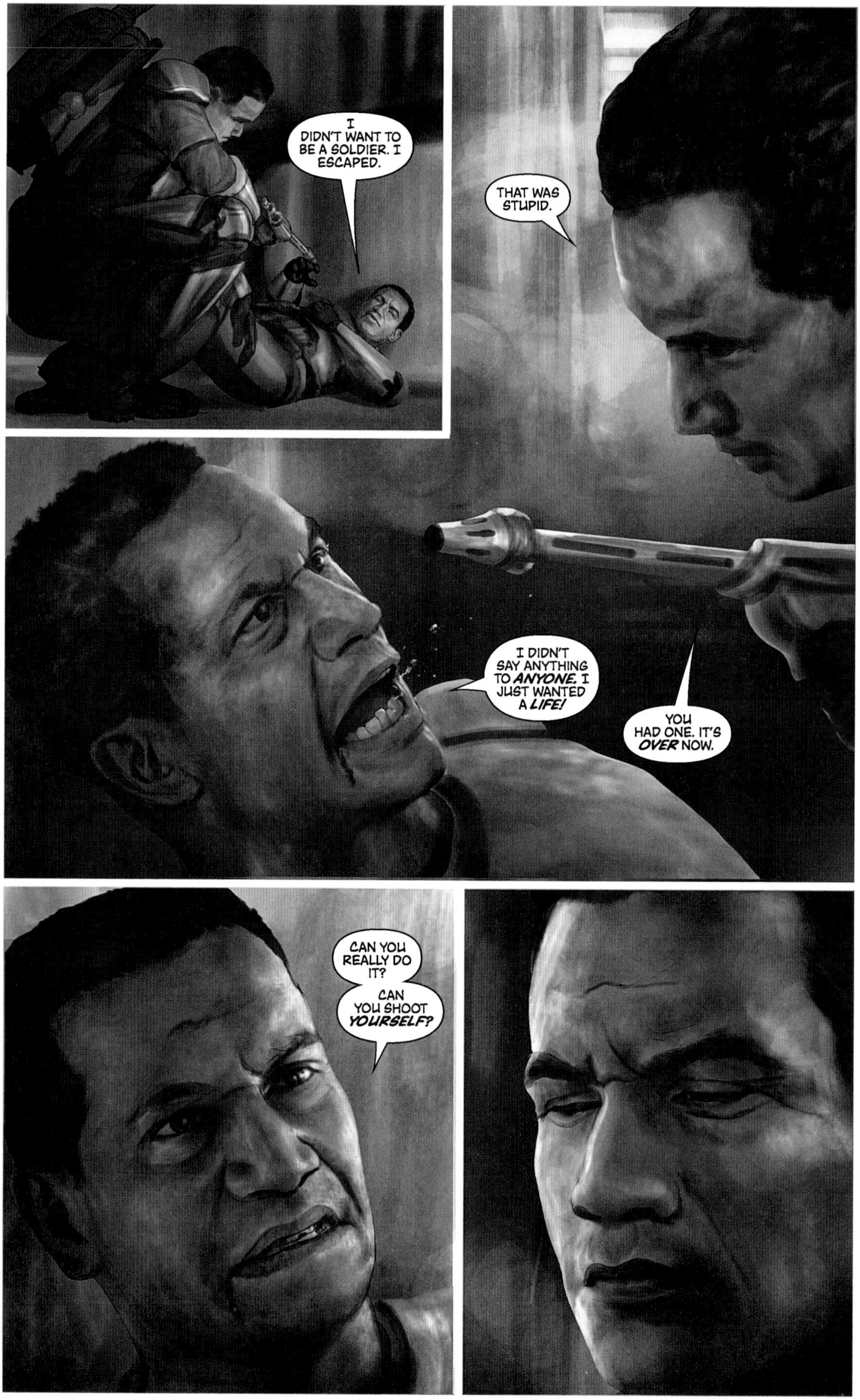
I DIDN'T WANT TO BE A SOLDIER. I ESCAPED.
THAT WAS STUPID.
I DIDN'T SAY ANYTHING TO *ANYONE*. I JUST WANTED A *LIFE!*
YOU HAD ONE. IT'S *OVER* NOW.
CAN YOU REALLY DO IT?
CAN YOU SHOOT *YOURSELF?*

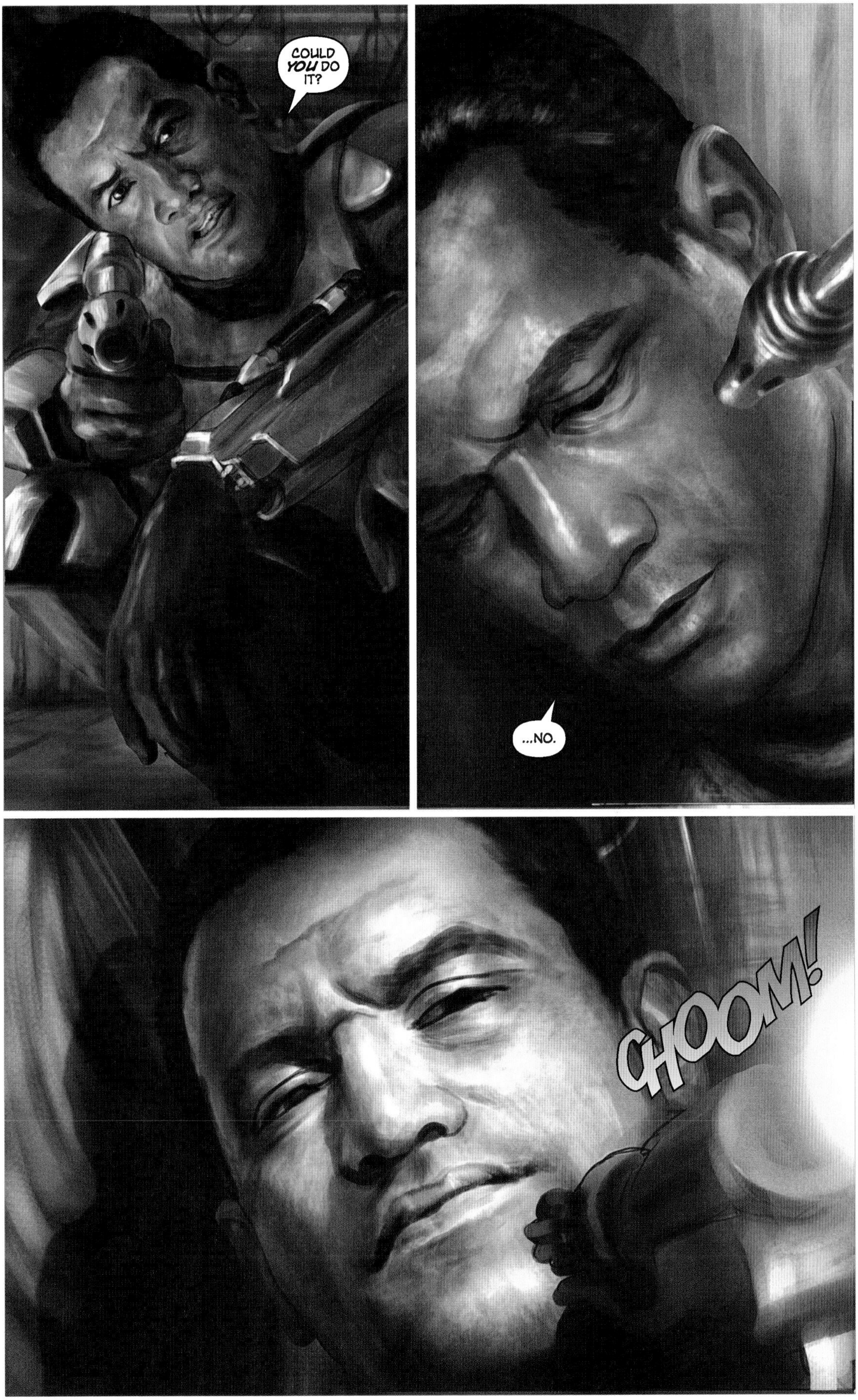
COULD *YOU* DO IT?
...NO.
CHOOM!

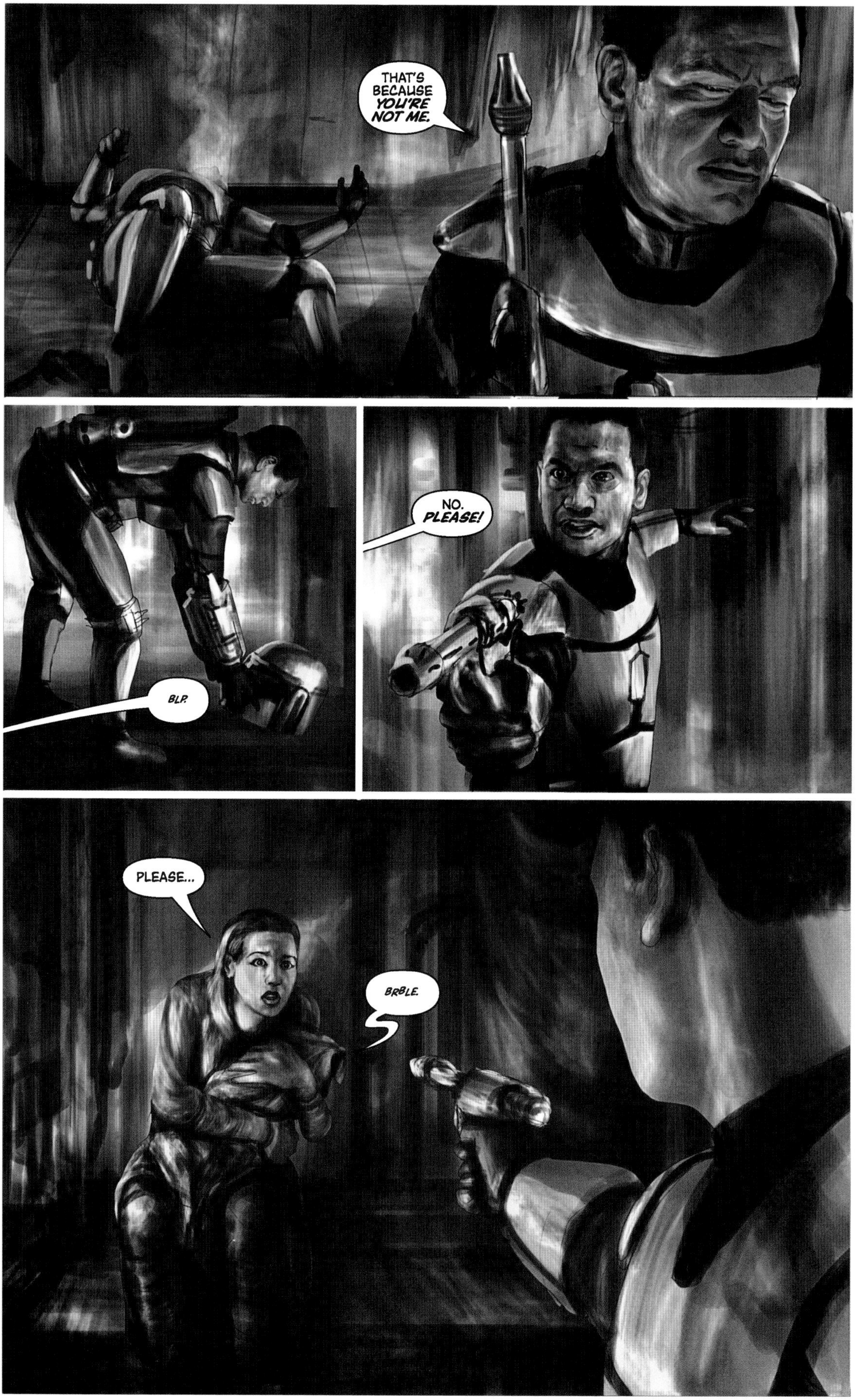
THAT'S BECAUSE *YOU'RE NOT ME.*
BLP.
NO. *PLEASE!*
PLEASE...
BRBLE.

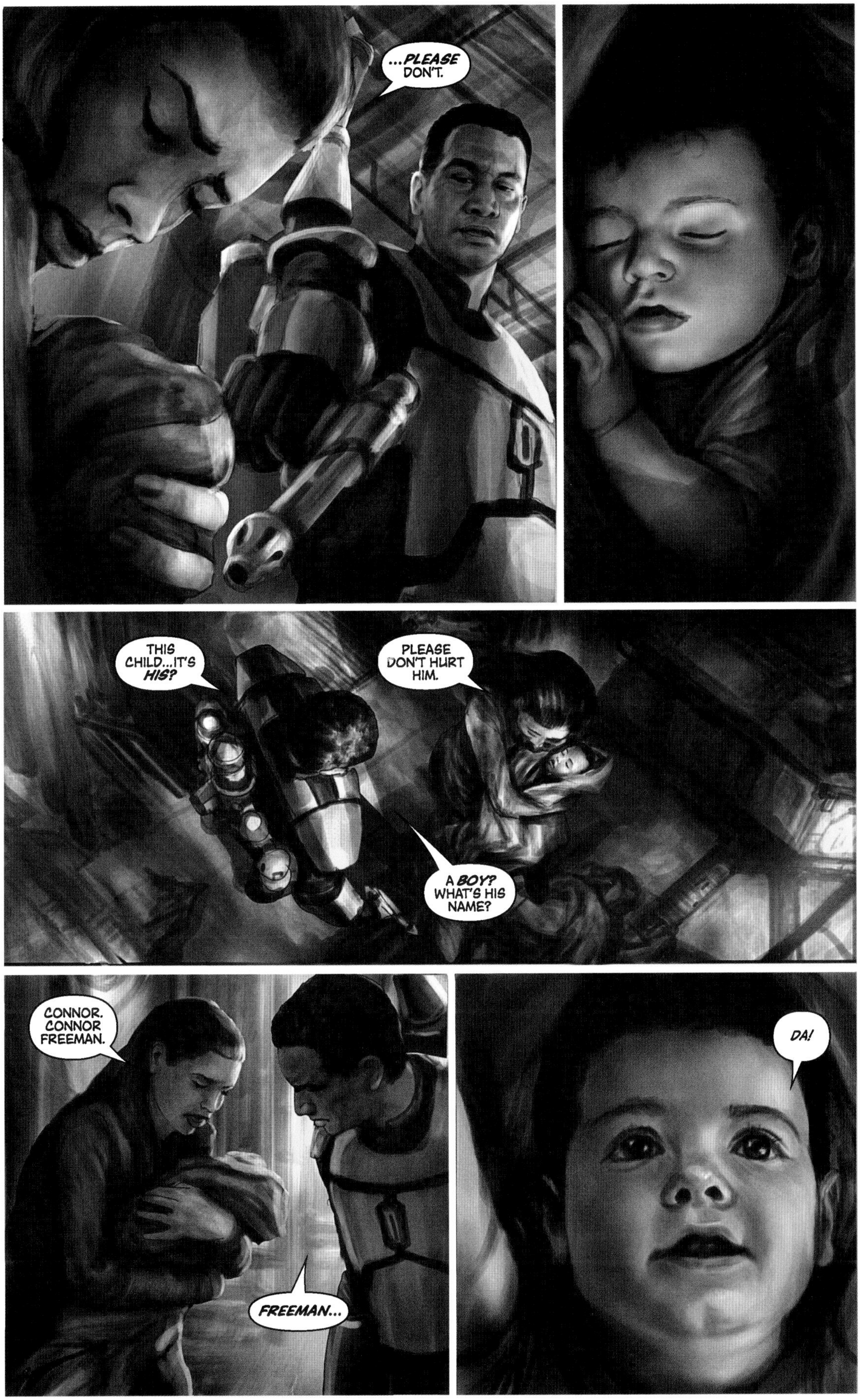

...PLEASE DON'T.
THIS CHILD...IT'S HIS?
PLEASE DON'T HURT HIM.
A BOY? WHAT'S HIS NAME?
CONNOR. CONNOR FREEMAN.
FREEMAN...
DA!

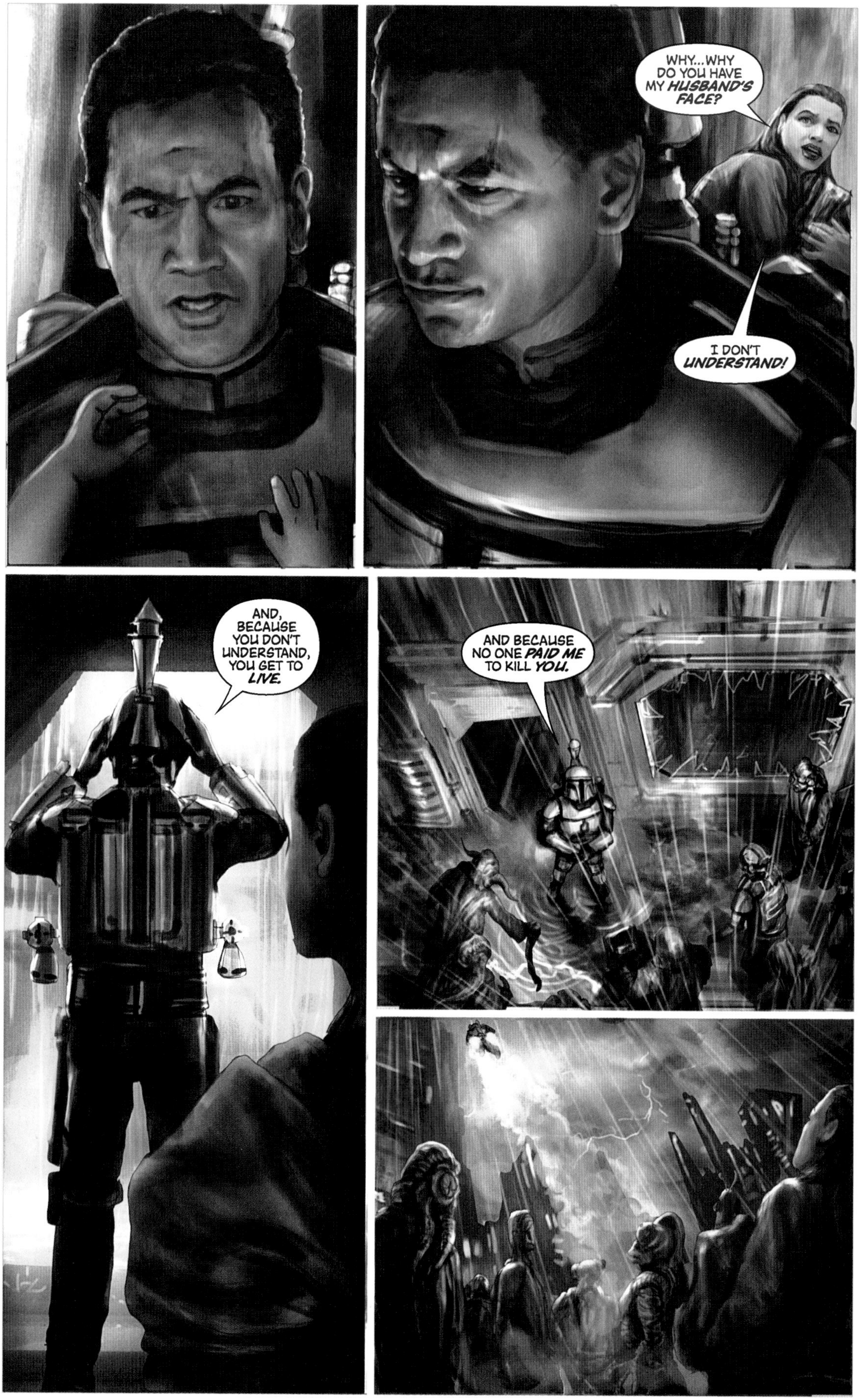
WHY...WHY DO YOU HAVE MY HUSBAND'S FACE?
I DON'T UNDERSTAND!
AND, BECAUSE YOU DON'T UNDERSTAND, YOU GET TO LIVE.
AND BECAUSE NO ONE PAID ME TO KILL YOU.

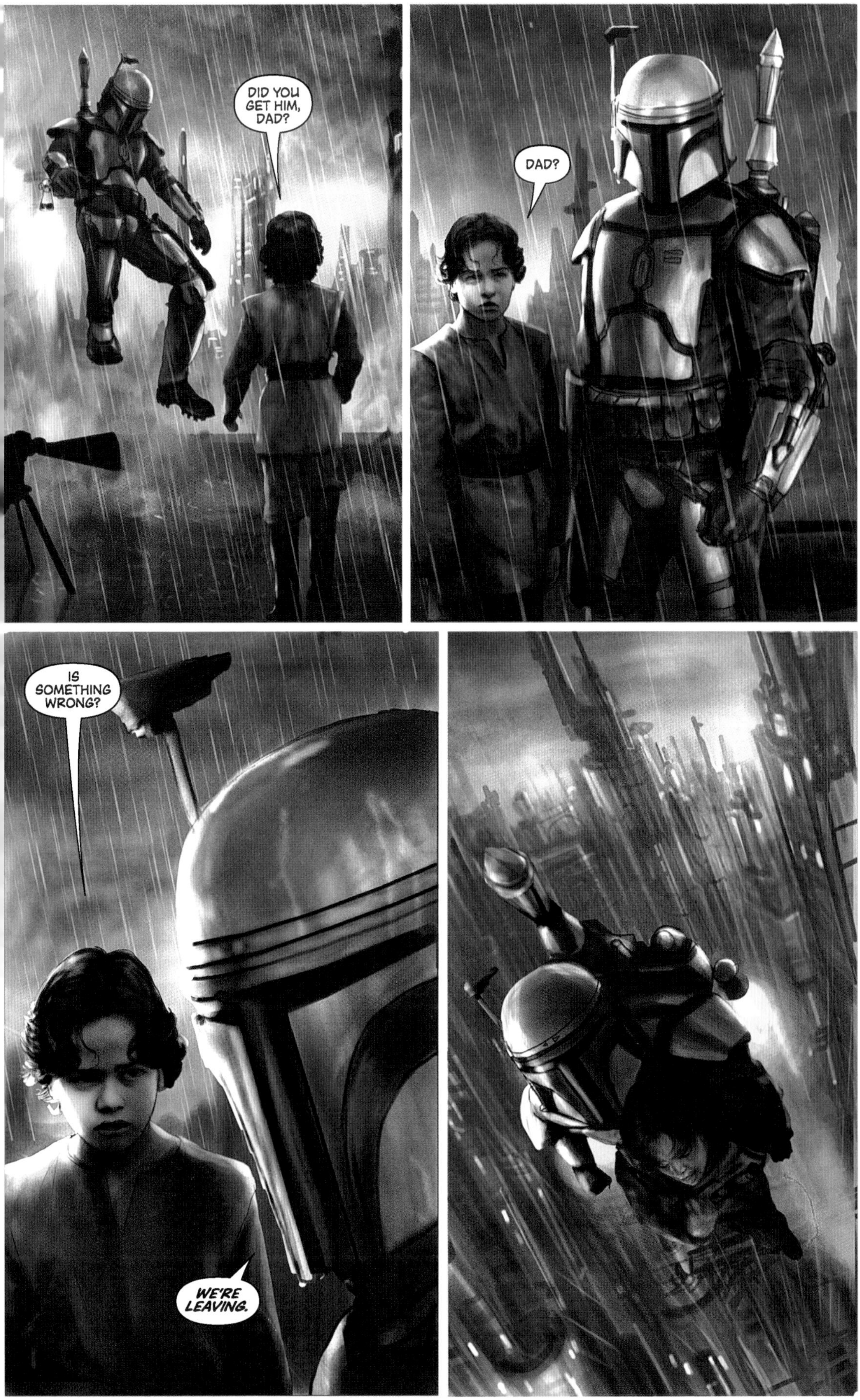
DID YOU GET HIM, DAD?
DAD?
IS SOMETHING WRONG?
WE'RE LEAVING.

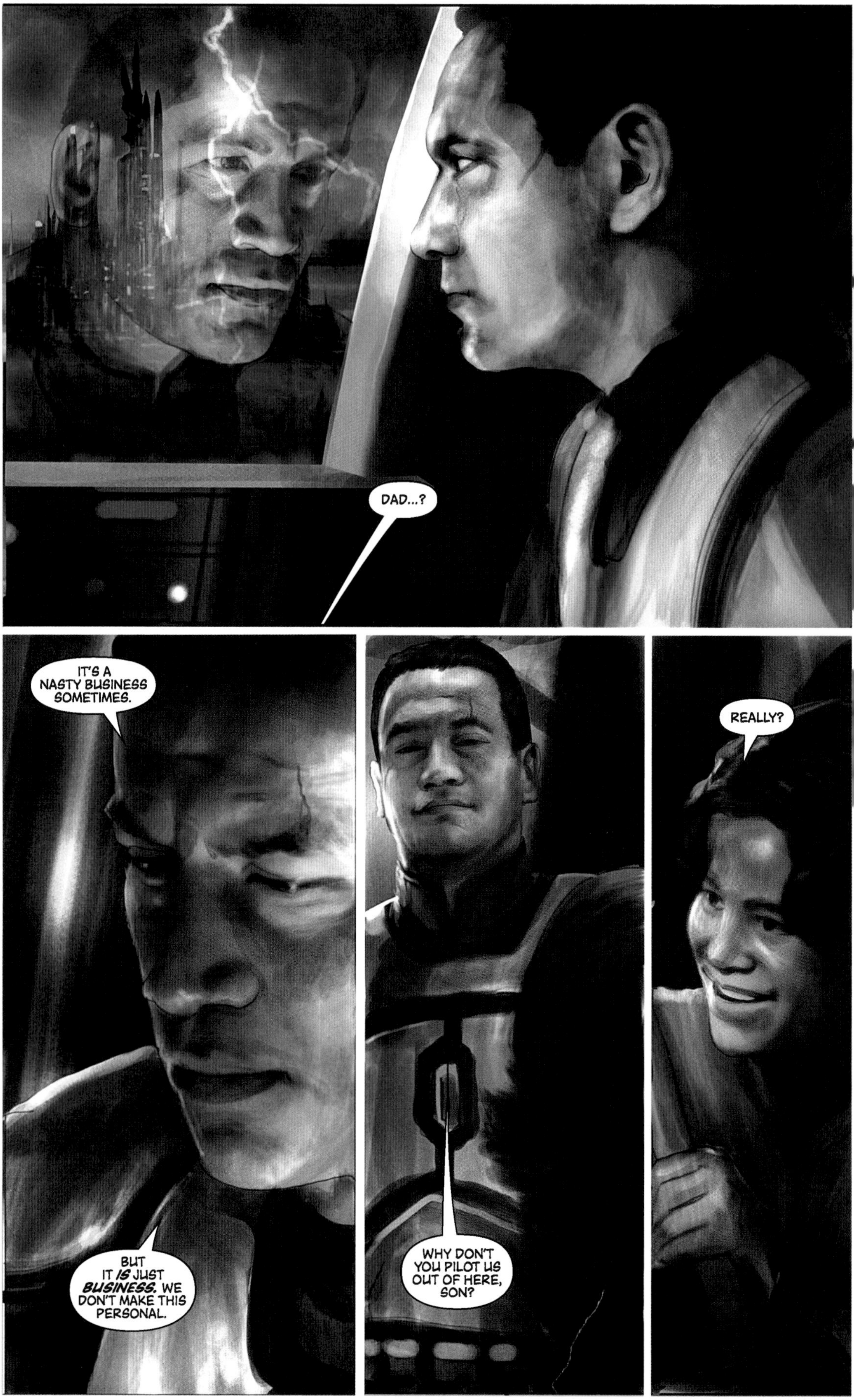
DAD...?
IT'S A NASTY BUSINESS SOMETIMES.
BUT IT *IS* JUST ***BUSINESS.*** WE DON'T MAKE THIS PERSONAL.
WHY DON'T YOU PILOT US OUT OF HERE, SON?
REALLY?

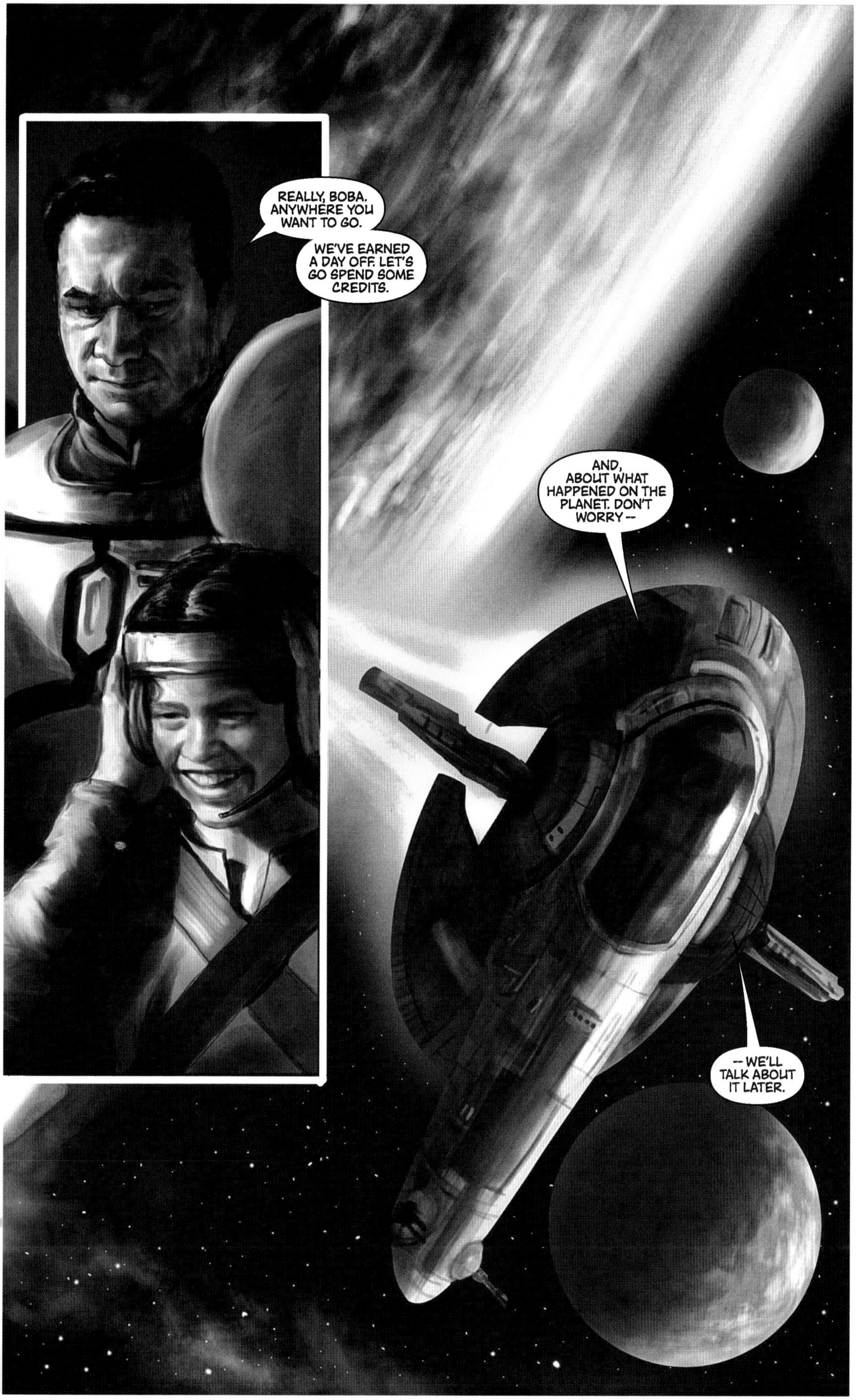
REALLY, BOBA. ANYWHERE YOU WANT TO GO.
WE'VE EARNED A DAY OFF. LET'S GO SPEND SOME CREDITS.
AND, ABOUT WHAT HAPPENED ON THE PLANET. DON'T WORRY --
-- WE'LL TALK ABOUT IT LATER.

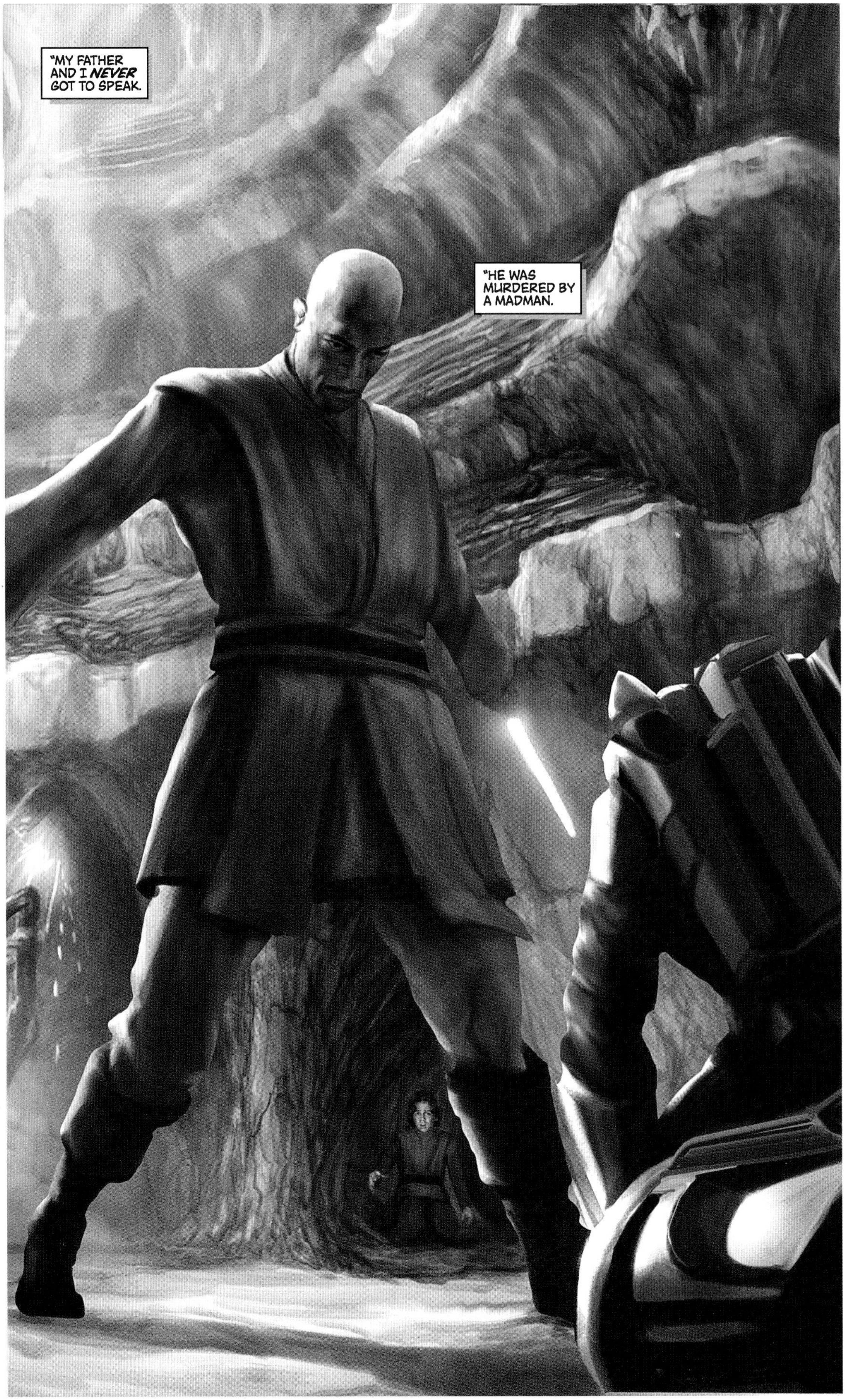
"MY FATHER AND I *NEVER* GOT TO SPEAK.
"HE WAS MURDERED BY A MADMAN.

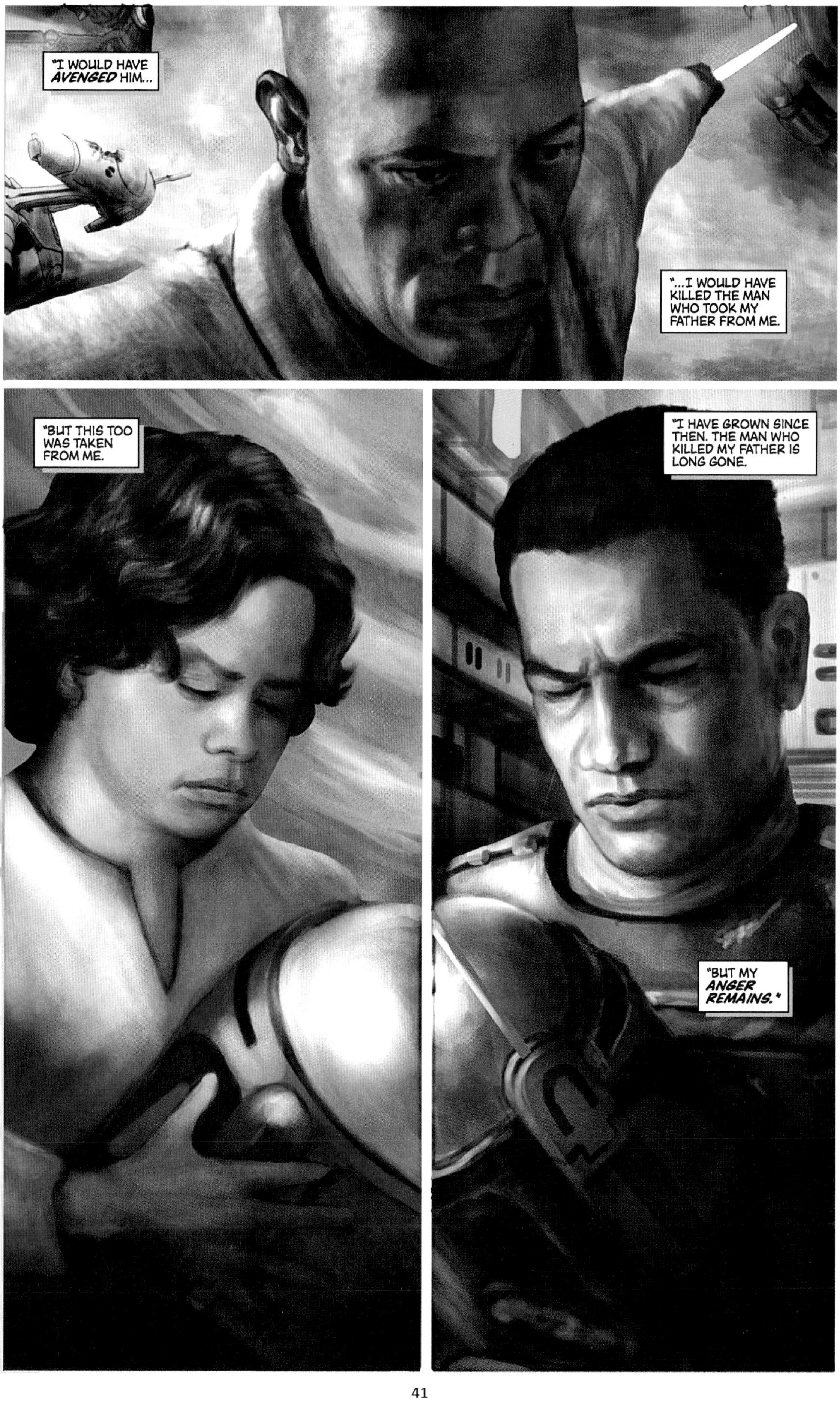
"I WOULD HAVE *AVENGED* HIM...
"...I WOULD HAVE KILLED THE MAN WHO TOOK MY FATHER FROM ME.
"BUT THIS TOO WAS TAKEN FROM ME.
"I HAVE GROWN SINCE THEN. THE MAN WHO KILLED MY FATHER IS LONG GONE.
"BUT MY *ANGER REMAINS.*"

WHAT HAVE YOU GOT FOR ME?

IT'S GOOD TO SEE *YOU* TOO, BOBA FETT.

I HAVE NO PATIENCE TODAY, GILEAN. *BOUNTIES.*

THERE ARE A NUMBER OF BOUNTIES THAT MAY INTEREST YOU. BUT I THOUGHT, AS YOUR BANKER, THAT I SHOULD ALERT YOU TO ONE IN PARTICULAR...

THIS BOUNTY IS ON A MAN CALLED *CONNOR FREEMAN.*

THAT'S NOT A LARGE BOUNTY...

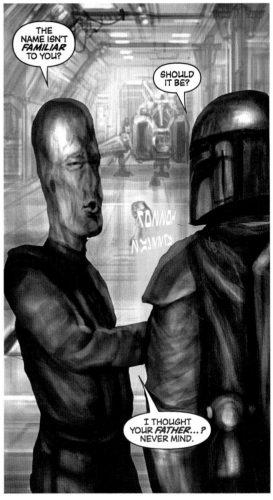

THE NAME ISN'T *FAMILIAR* TO YOU?

SHOULD IT BE?

I THOUGHT YOUR *FATHER...?* NEVER MIND.

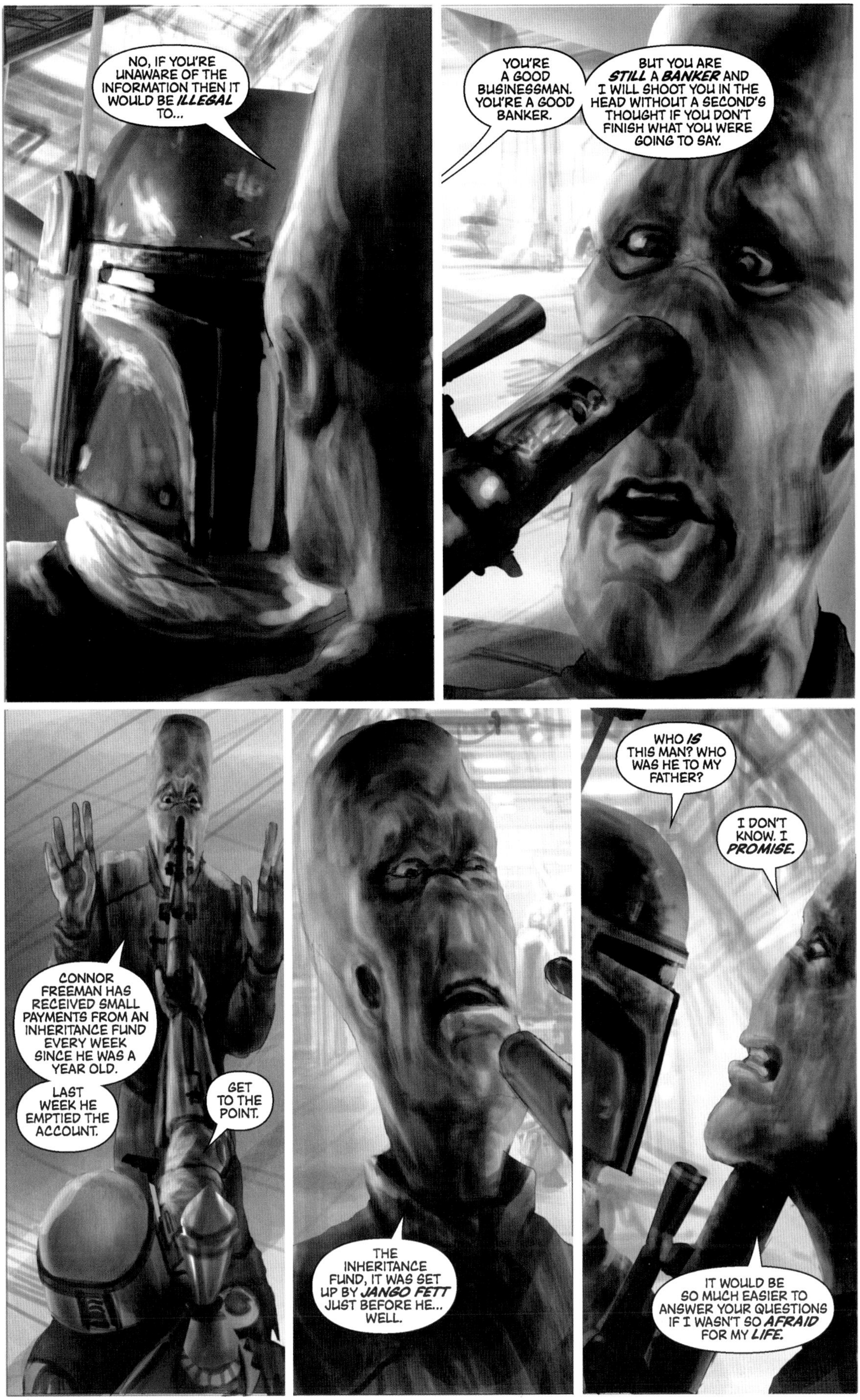
NO, IF YOU'RE UNAWARE OF THE INFORMATION THEN IT WOULD BE *ILLEGAL* TO...
YOU'RE A GOOD BUSINESSMAN. YOU'RE A GOOD BANKER.
BUT YOU ARE *STILL* A *BANKER* AND I WILL SHOOT YOU IN THE HEAD WITHOUT A SECOND'S THOUGHT IF YOU DON'T FINISH WHAT YOU WERE GOING TO SAY.
CONNOR FREEMAN HAS RECEIVED SMALL PAYMENTS FROM AN INHERITANCE FUND EVERY WEEK SINCE HE WAS A YEAR OLD.
LAST WEEK HE EMPTIED THE ACCOUNT.
GET TO THE POINT.
THE INHERITANCE FUND, IT WAS SET UP BY *JANGO FETT* JUST BEFORE HE... WELL.
WHO *IS* THIS MAN? WHO WAS HE TO MY FATHER?
I DON'T KNOW. I *PROMISE.*
IT WOULD BE SO MUCH EASIER TO ANSWER YOUR QUESTIONS IF I WASN'T SO *AFRAID* FOR MY *LIFE.*

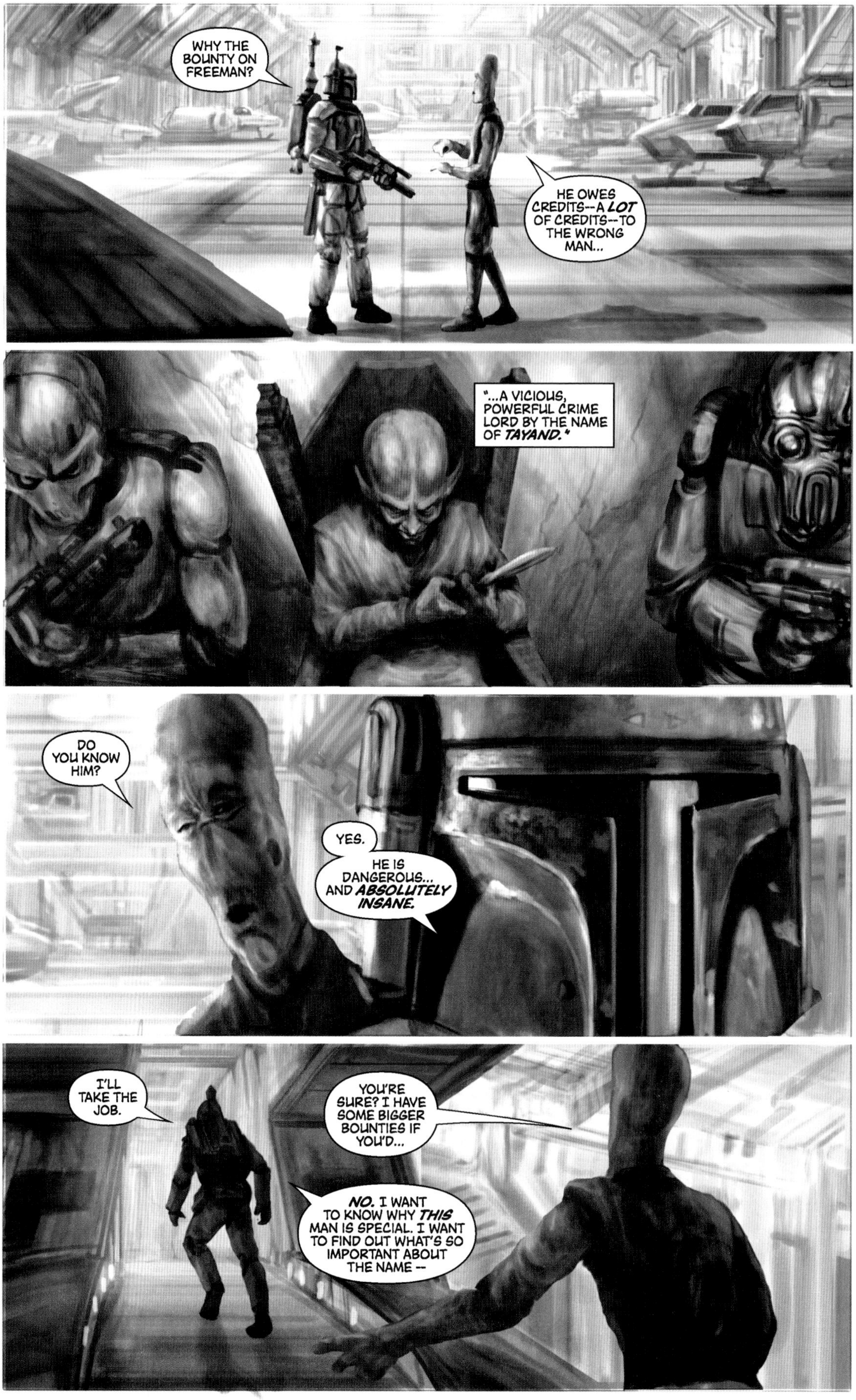
WHY THE BOUNTY ON FREEMAN?
HE OWES CREDITS--A LOT OF CREDITS--TO THE WRONG MAN...
"...A VICIOUS, POWERFUL CRIME LORD BY THE NAME OF TAYAND."
DO YOU KNOW HIM?
YES.
HE IS DANGEROUS... AND ABSOLUTELY INSANE.
I'LL TAKE THE JOB.
YOU'RE SURE? I HAVE SOME BIGGER BOUNTIES IF YOU'D...
NO. I WANT TO KNOW WHY THIS MAN IS SPECIAL. I WANT TO FIND OUT WHAT'S SO IMPORTANT ABOUT THE NAME --

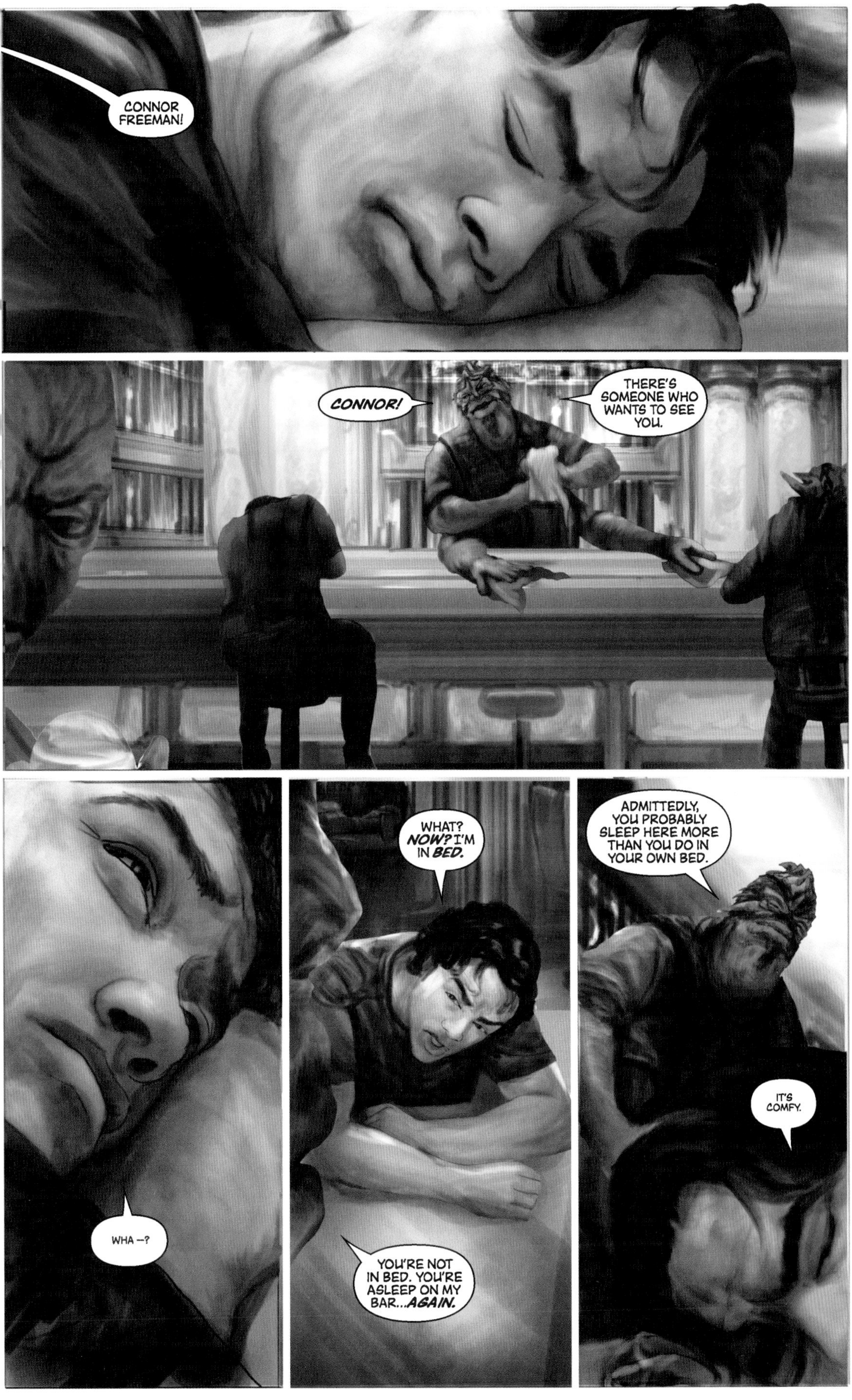

CONNOR FREEMAN!
CONNOR!
THERE'S SOMEONE WHO WANTS TO SEE YOU.
WHA —?
WHAT? NOW? I'M IN BED.
YOU'RE NOT IN BED. YOU'RE ASLEEP ON MY BAR...AGAIN.
ADMITTEDLY, YOU PROBABLY SLEEP HERE MORE THAN YOU DO IN YOUR OWN BED.
IT'S COMFY.

CONNOR FREEMAN?

GO AWAY--

--CAN'T YOU SEE I'M IN BED?

YOU'RE WORTH QUITE A BIT OF MONEY, SO *WAKE UP.*

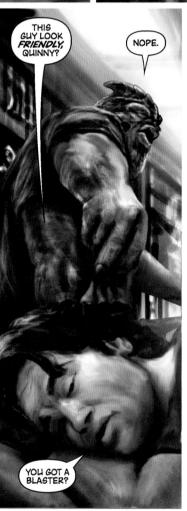

THIS GUY LOOK *FRIENDLY,* QUINNY?

NOPE.

YOU GOT A BLASTER?

YEP.

46

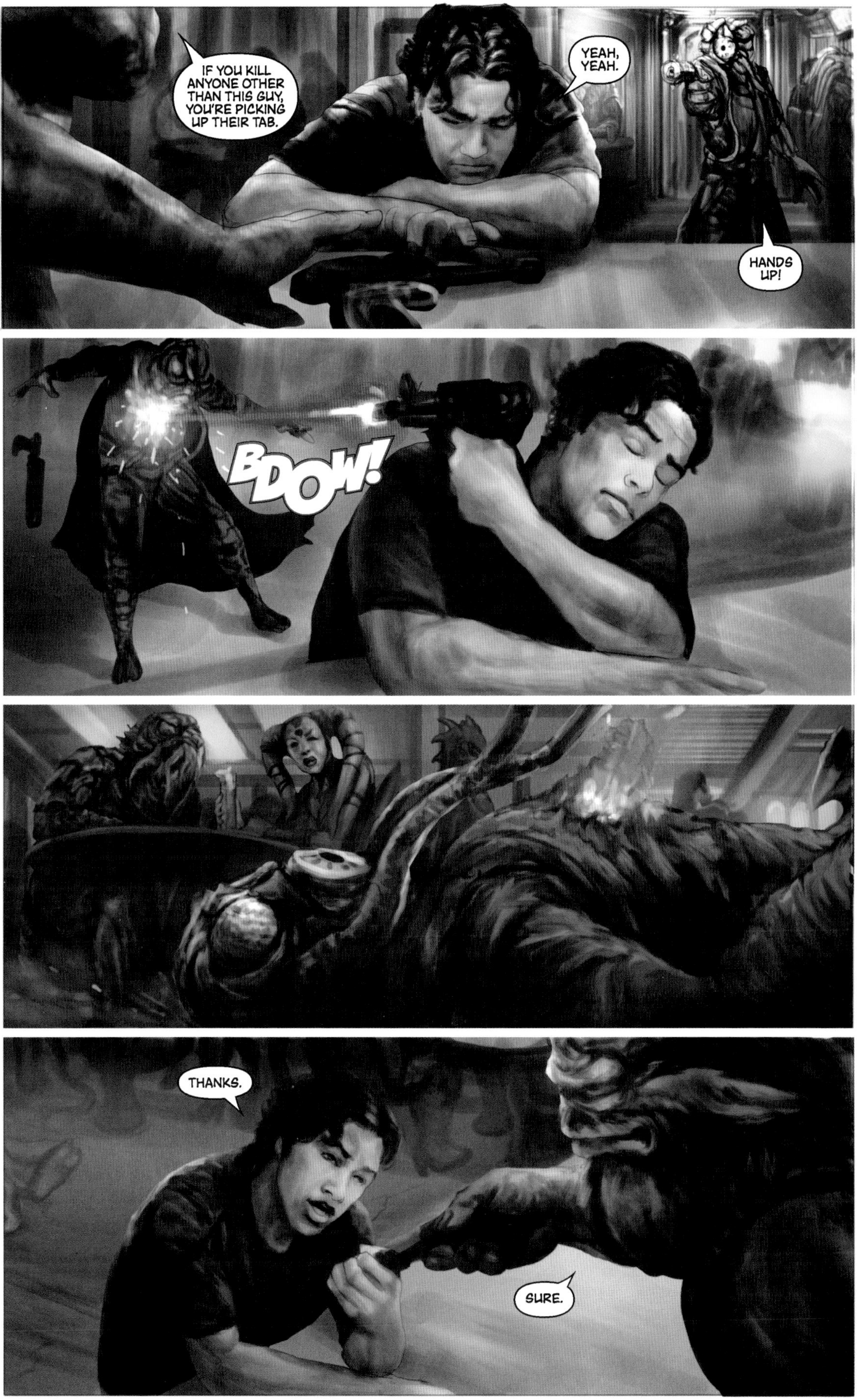
IF YOU KILL ANYONE OTHER THAN THIS GUY, YOU'RE PICKING UP THEIR TAB.
YEAH, YEAH.
HANDS UP!
BDOW!
THANKS.
SURE.

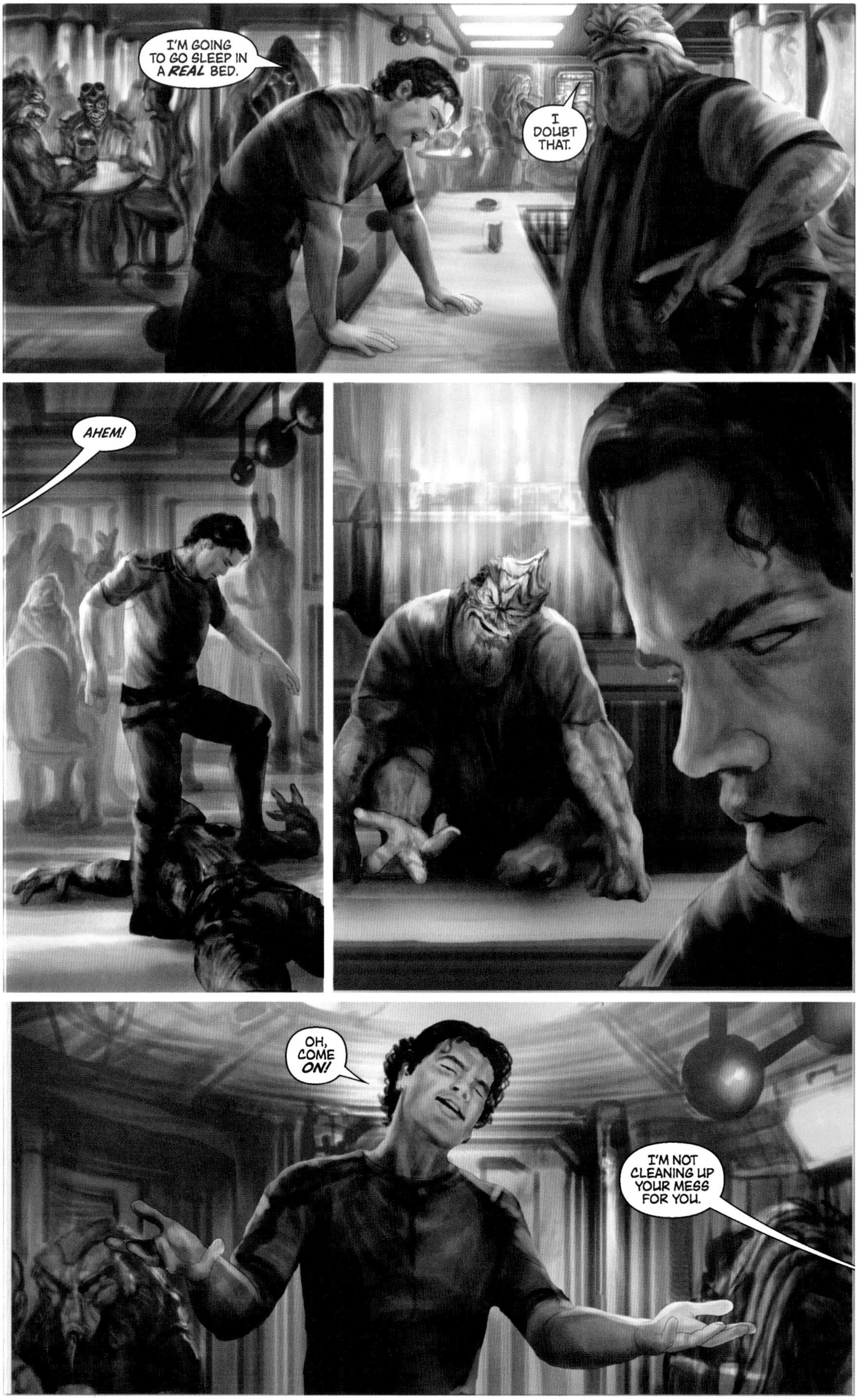
I'M GOING TO GO SLEEP IN A *REAL* BED.
I DOUBT THAT.
AHEM!
OH, COME *ON!*
I'M NOT CLEANING UP YOUR MESS FOR YOU.

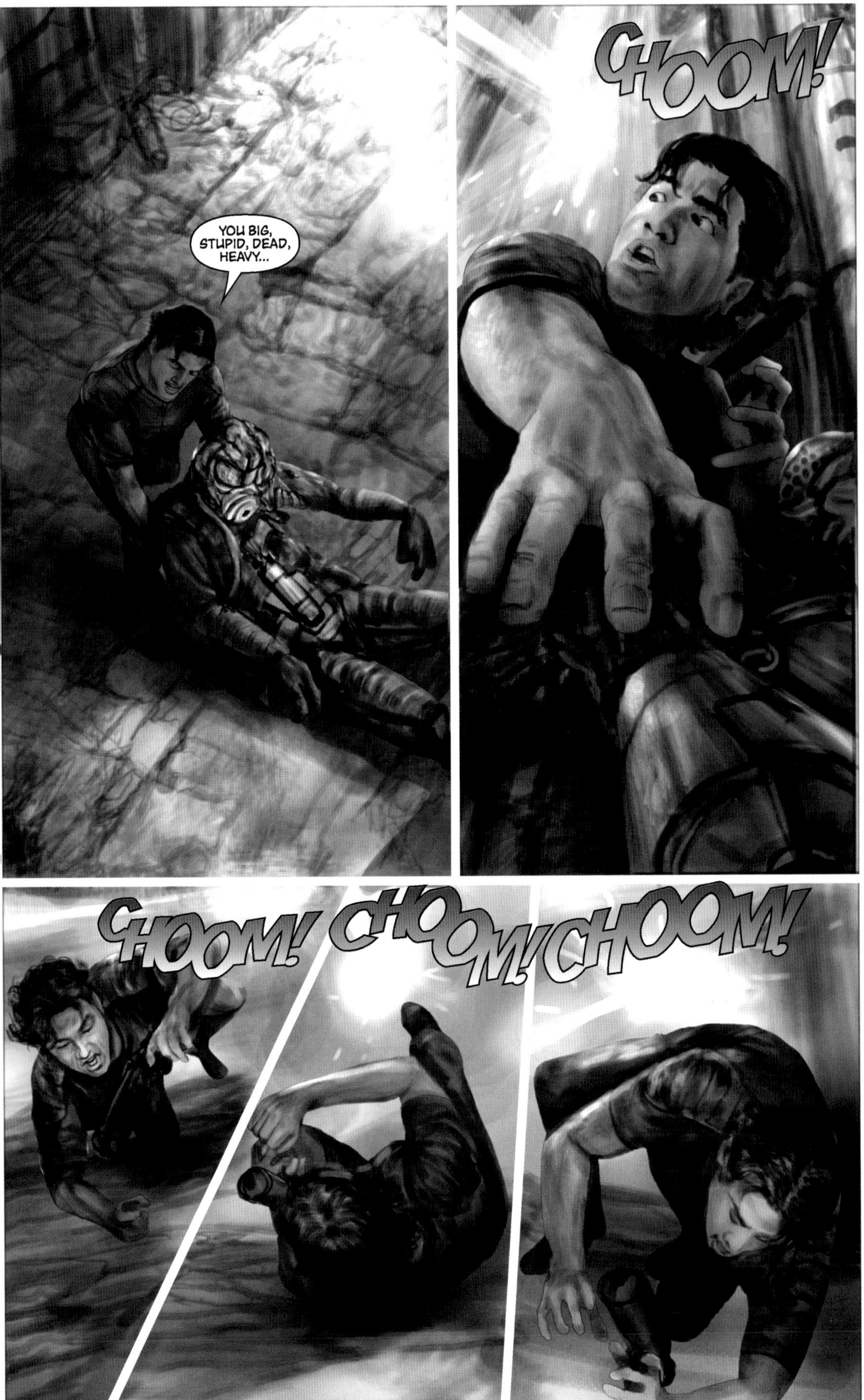
YOU BIG, STUPID, DEAD, HEAVY...
CHOOM!
CHOOM! CHOOM! CHOOM!

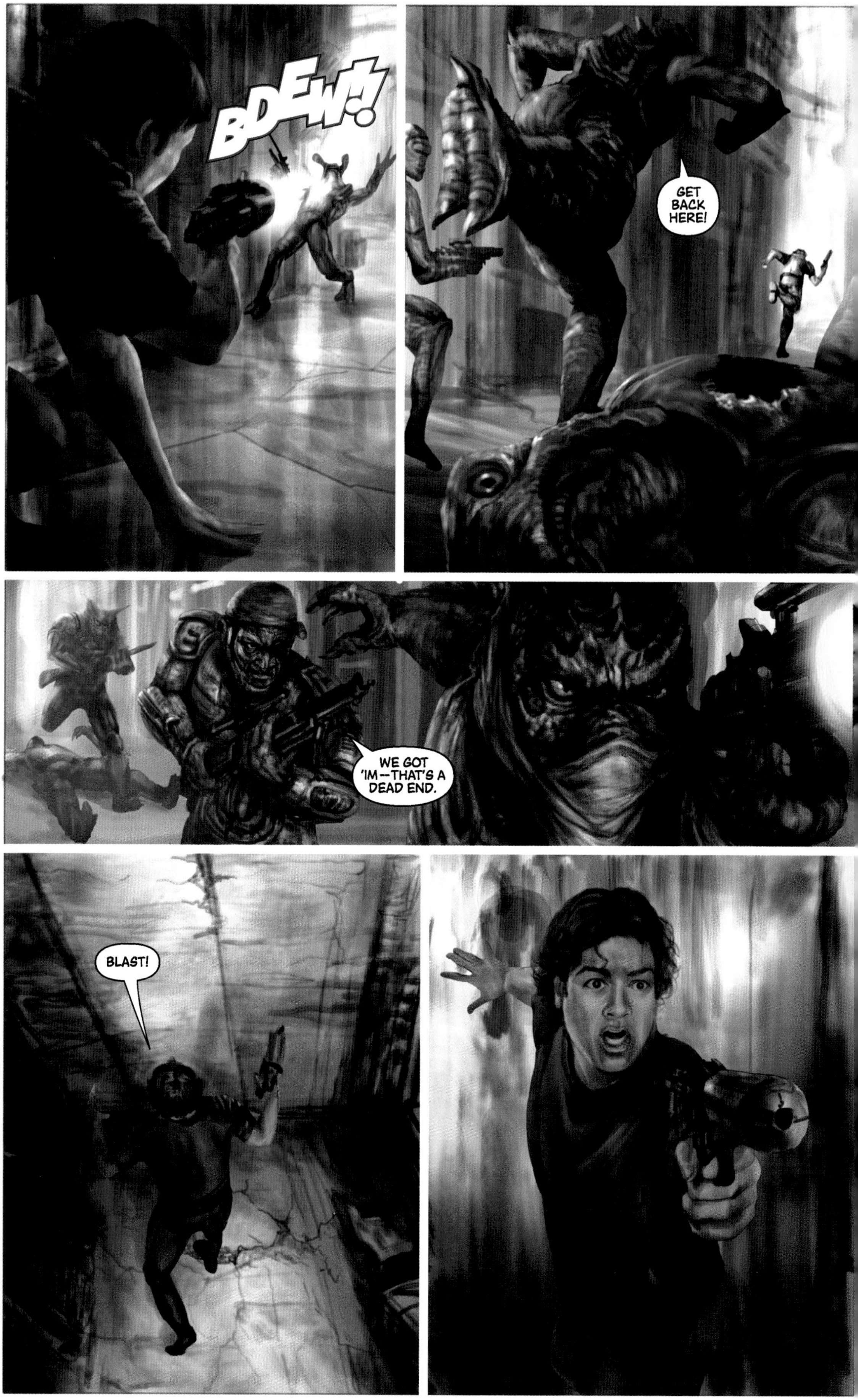
BDEW!!
GET BACK HERE!
WE GOT 'IM--THAT'S A DEAD END.
BLAST!

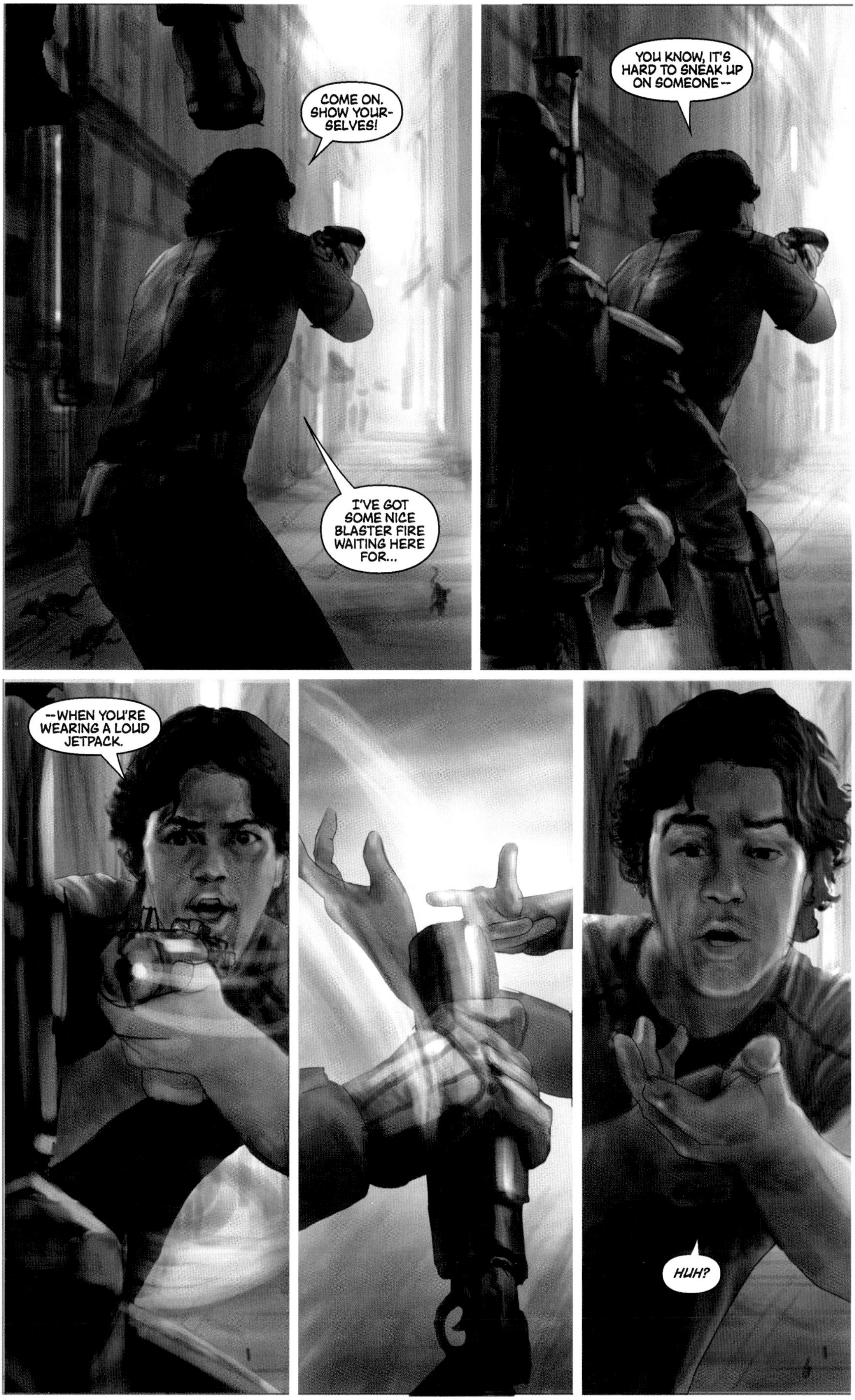
COME ON. SHOW YOUR-SELVES!
I'VE GOT SOME NICE BLASTER FIRE WAITING HERE FOR...
YOU KNOW, IT'S HARD TO SNEAK UP ON SOMEONE--
--WHEN YOU'RE WEARING A LOUD JETPACK.
HUH?

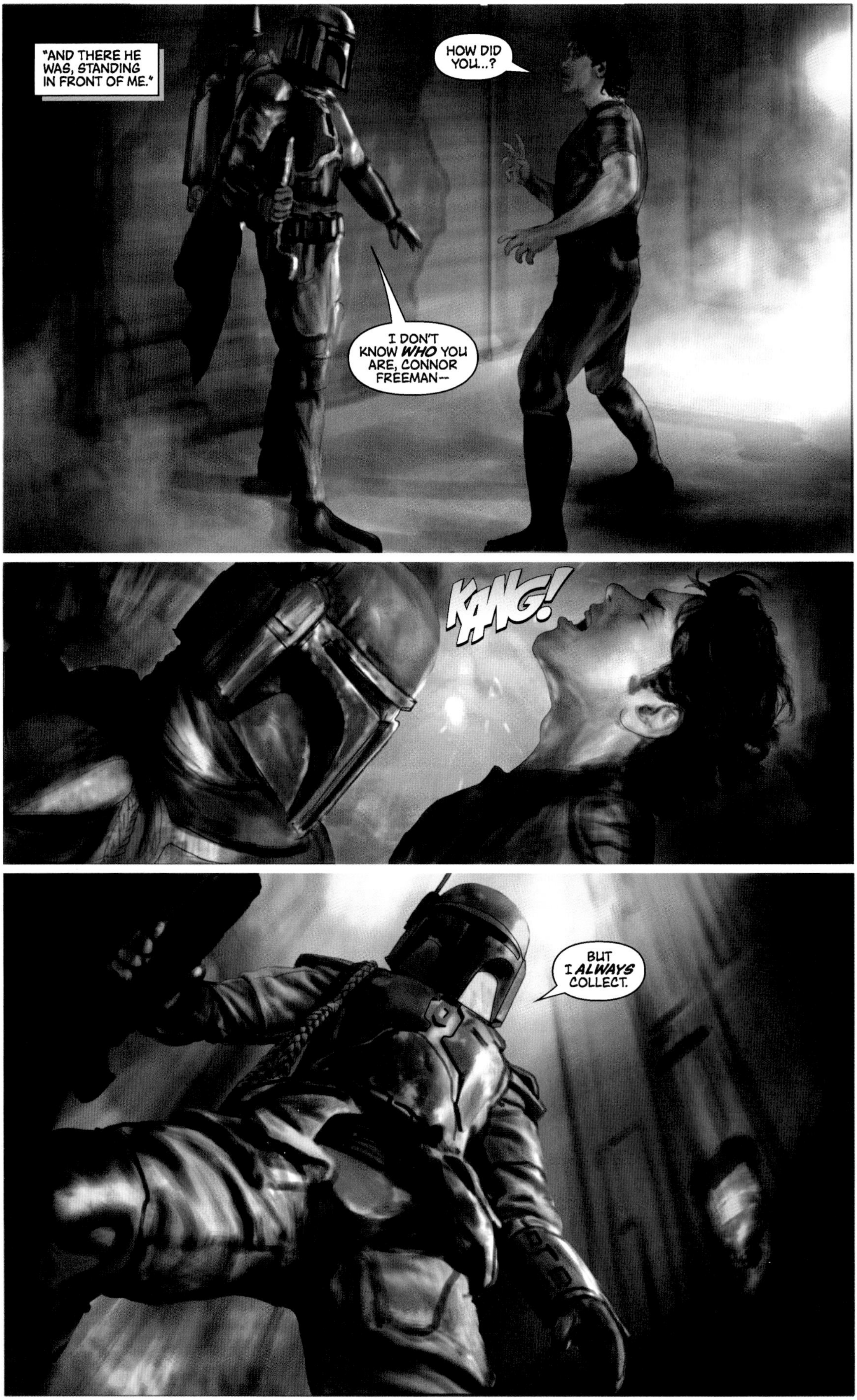
"AND THERE HE WAS, STANDING IN FRONT OF ME."
HOW DID YOU...?
I DON'T KNOW WHO YOU ARE, CONNOR FREEMAN--
KANG!
BUT I ALWAYS COLLECT.

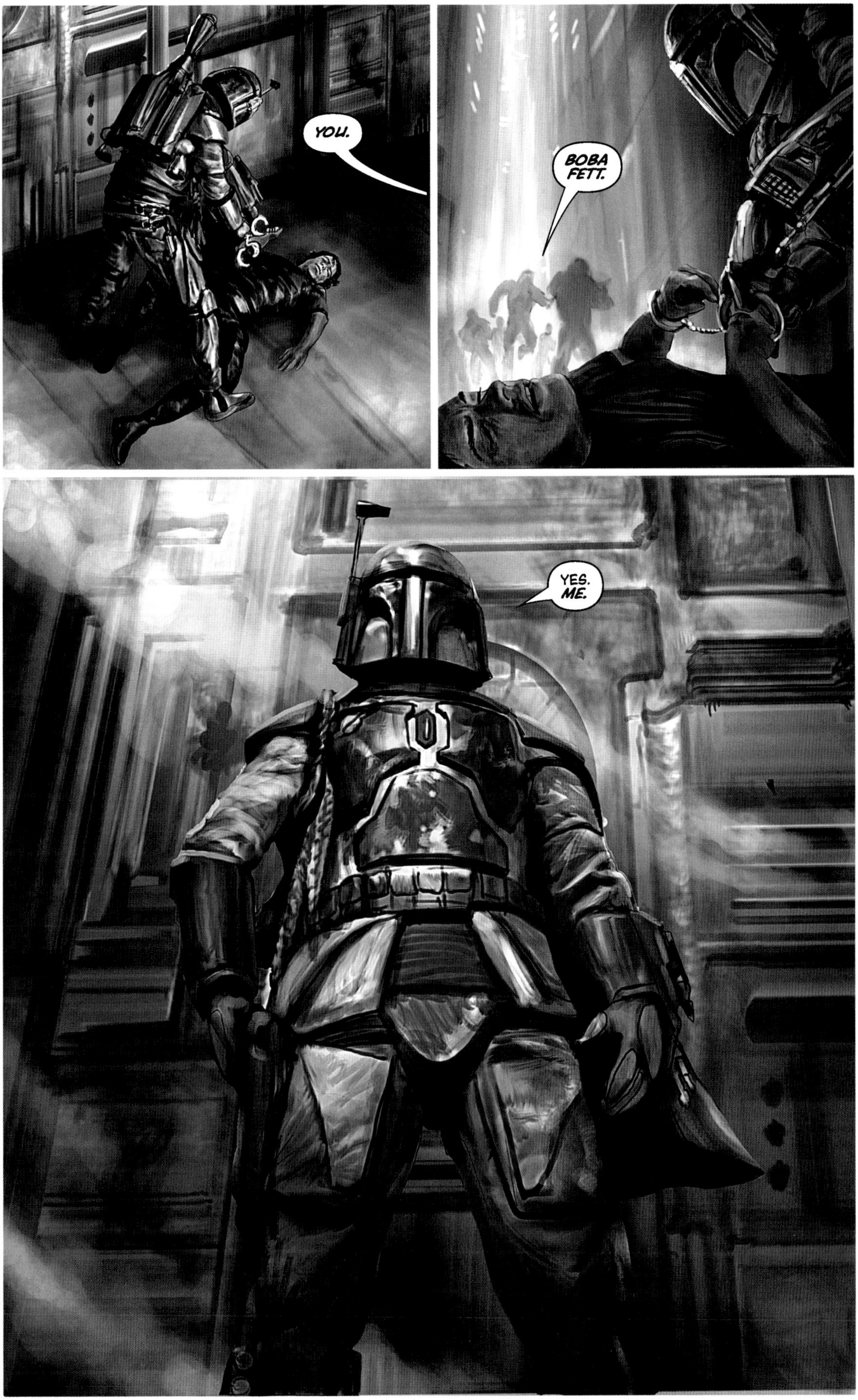
YOU.
BOBA FETT.
YES. ME.

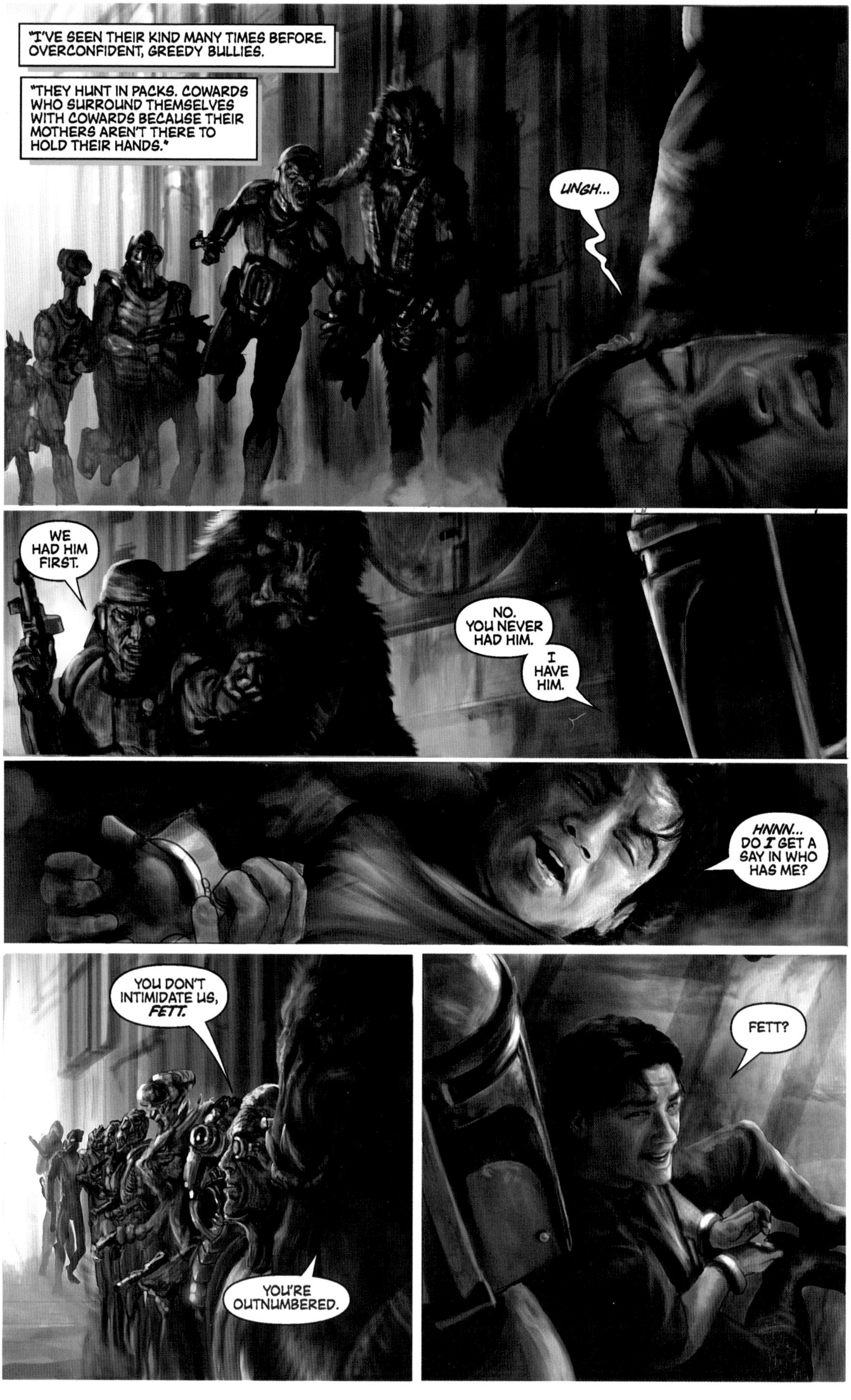

"I'VE SEEN THEIR KIND MANY TIMES BEFORE. OVERCONFIDENT, GREEDY BULLIES.
"THEY HUNT IN PACKS. COWARDS WHO SURROUND THEMSELVES WITH COWARDS BECAUSE THEIR MOTHERS AREN'T THERE TO HOLD THEIR HANDS."
UNGH...
WE HAD HIM FIRST.
NO. YOU NEVER HAD HIM.
I HAVE HIM.
HNNN... DO I GET A SAY IN WHO HAS ME?
YOU DON'T INTIMIDATE US, FETT.
YOU'RE OUTNUMBERED.
FETT?

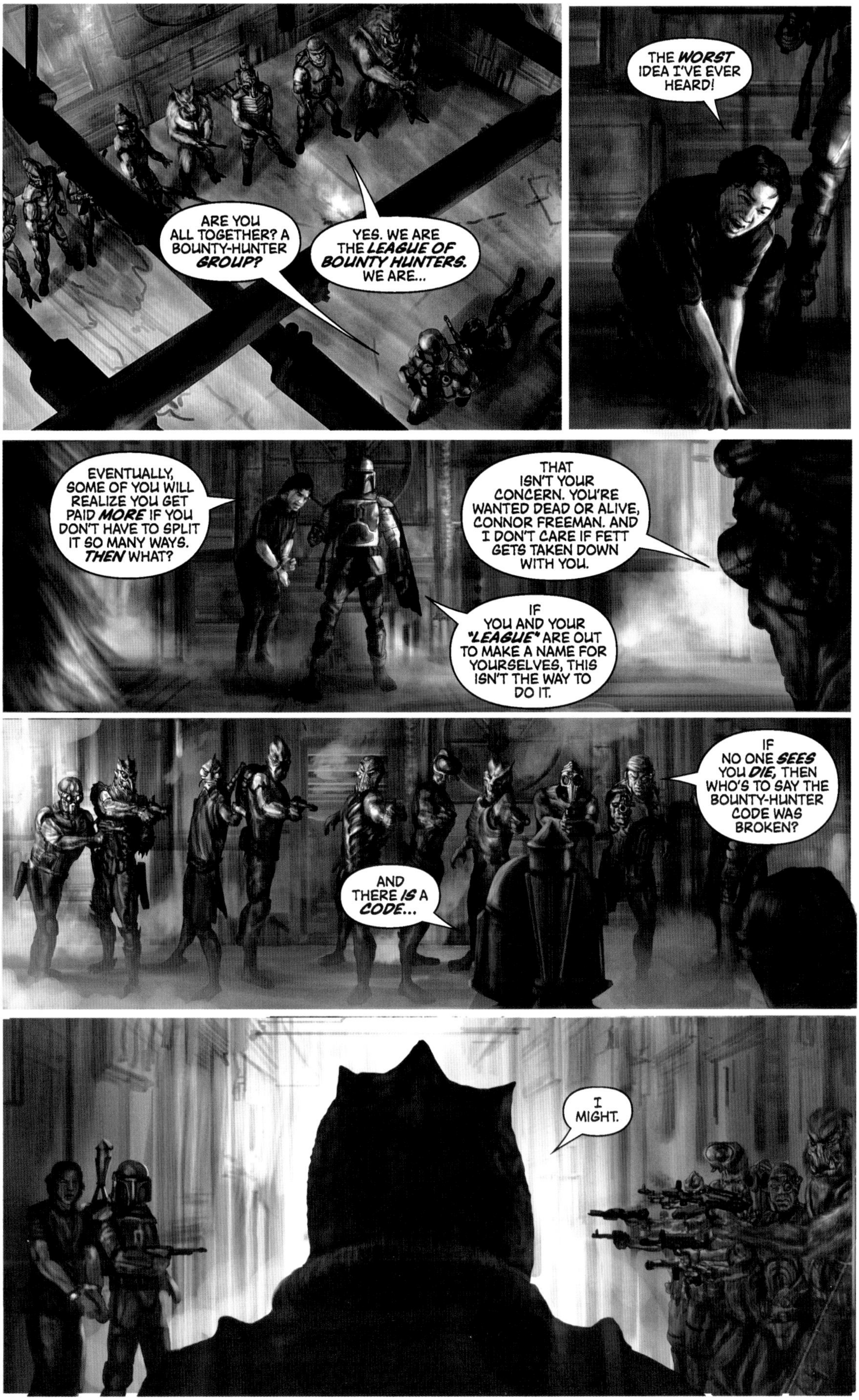
ARE YOU ALL TOGETHER? A BOUNTY-HUNTER GROUP?
YES. WE ARE THE LEAGUE OF BOUNTY HUNTERS. WE ARE...
THE WORST IDEA I'VE EVER HEARD!
EVENTUALLY, SOME OF YOU WILL REALIZE YOU GET PAID MORE IF YOU DON'T HAVE TO SPLIT IT SO MANY WAYS. THEN WHAT?
THAT ISN'T YOUR CONCERN. YOU'RE WANTED DEAD OR ALIVE, CONNOR FREEMAN. AND I DON'T CARE IF FETT GETS TAKEN DOWN WITH YOU.
IF YOU AND YOUR "LEAGUE" ARE OUT TO MAKE A NAME FOR YOURSELVES, THIS ISN'T THE WAY TO DO IT.
AND THERE IS A CODE...
IF NO ONE SEES YOU DIE, THEN WHO'S TO SAY THE BOUNTY-HUNTER CODE WAS BROKEN?
I MIGHT.

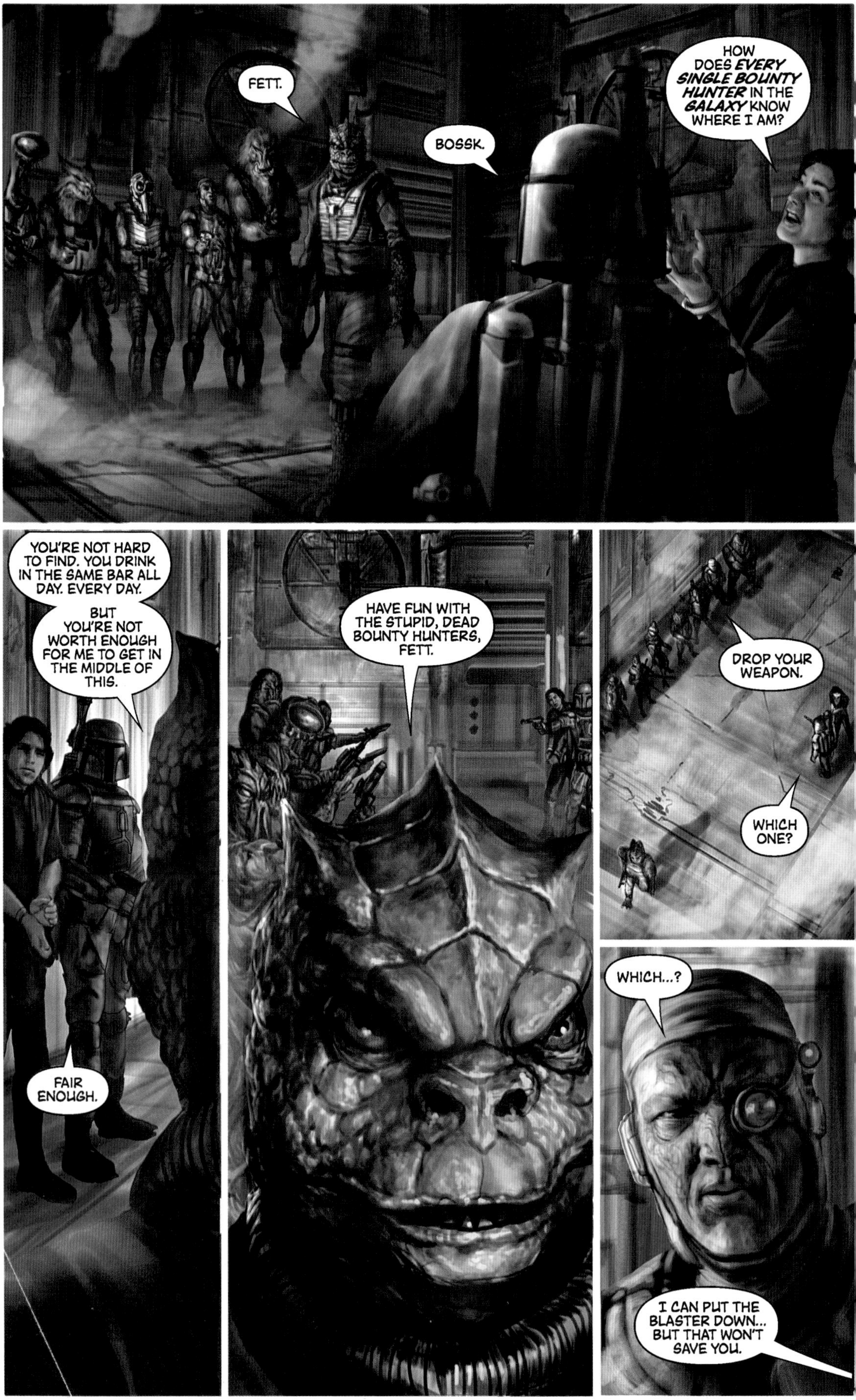

FETT.
BOSSK.
HOW DOES EVERY SINGLE BOUNTY HUNTER IN THE GALAXY KNOW WHERE I AM?
YOU'RE NOT HARD TO FIND. YOU DRINK IN THE SAME BAR ALL DAY. EVERY DAY.
BUT YOU'RE NOT WORTH ENOUGH FOR ME TO GET IN THE MIDDLE OF THIS.
FAIR ENOUGH.
HAVE FUN WITH THE STUPID, DEAD BOUNTY HUNTERS, FETT.
DROP YOUR WEAPON.
WHICH ONE?
WHICH...?
I CAN PUT THE BLASTER DOWN... BUT THAT WON'T SAVE YOU.

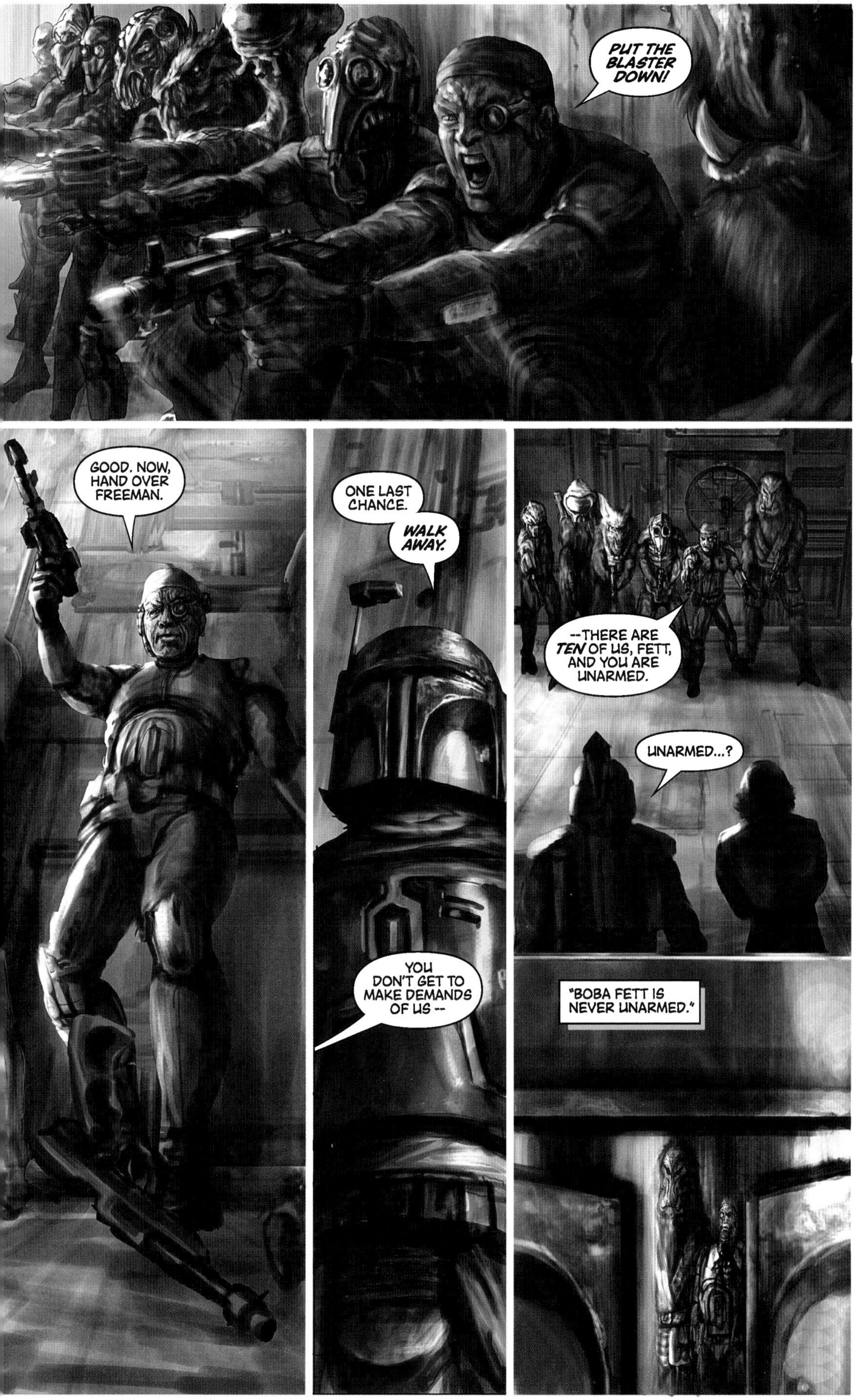
PUT THE BLASTER DOWN!
GOOD. NOW, HAND OVER FREEMAN.
ONE LAST CHANCE.
WALK AWAY.
YOU DON'T GET TO MAKE DEMANDS OF US --
--THERE ARE TEN OF US, FETT, AND YOU ARE UNARMED.
UNARMED...?
"BOBA FETT IS NEVER UNARMED."

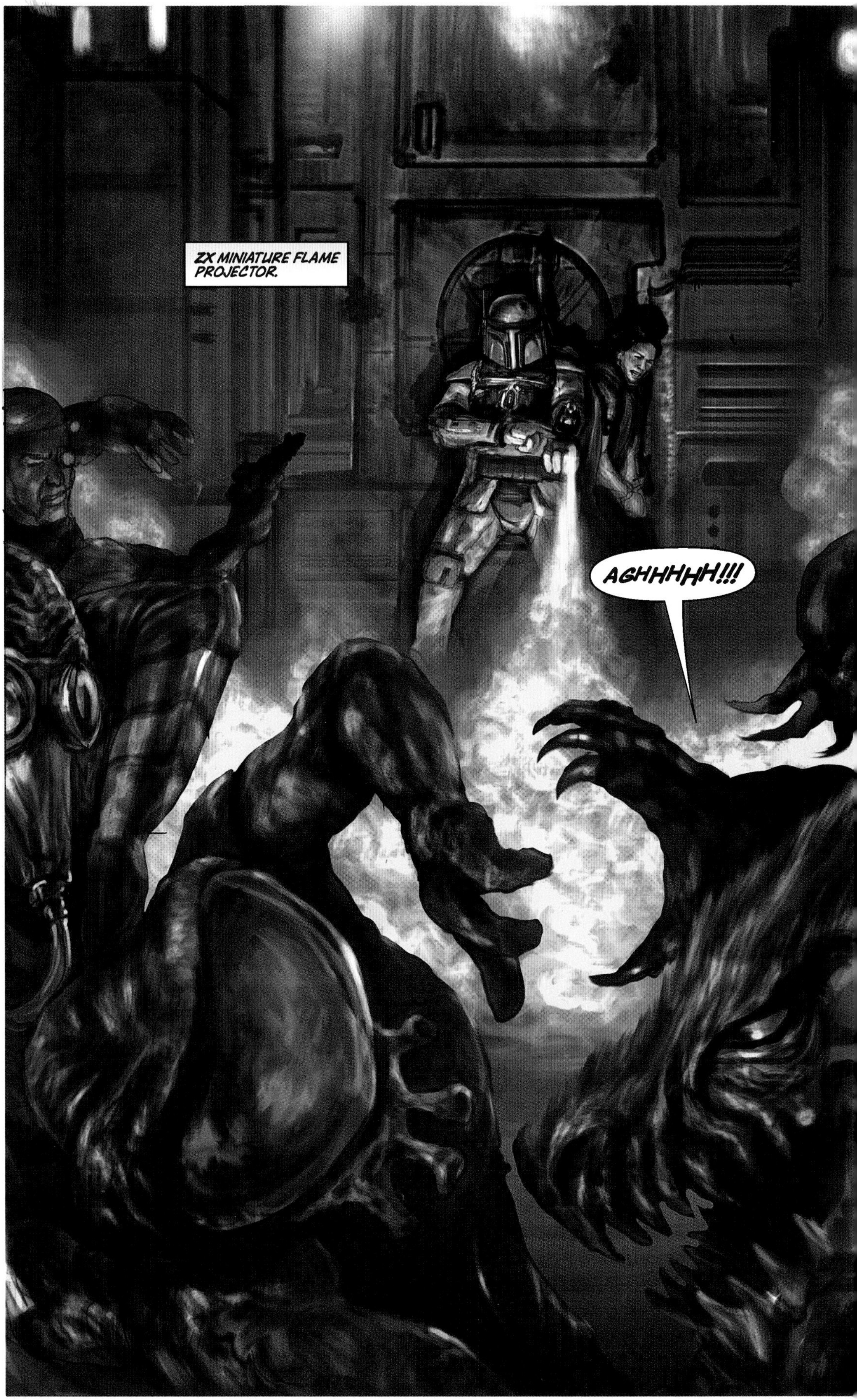
ZX MINIATURE FLAME PROJECTOR.
AGHHHHH!!!

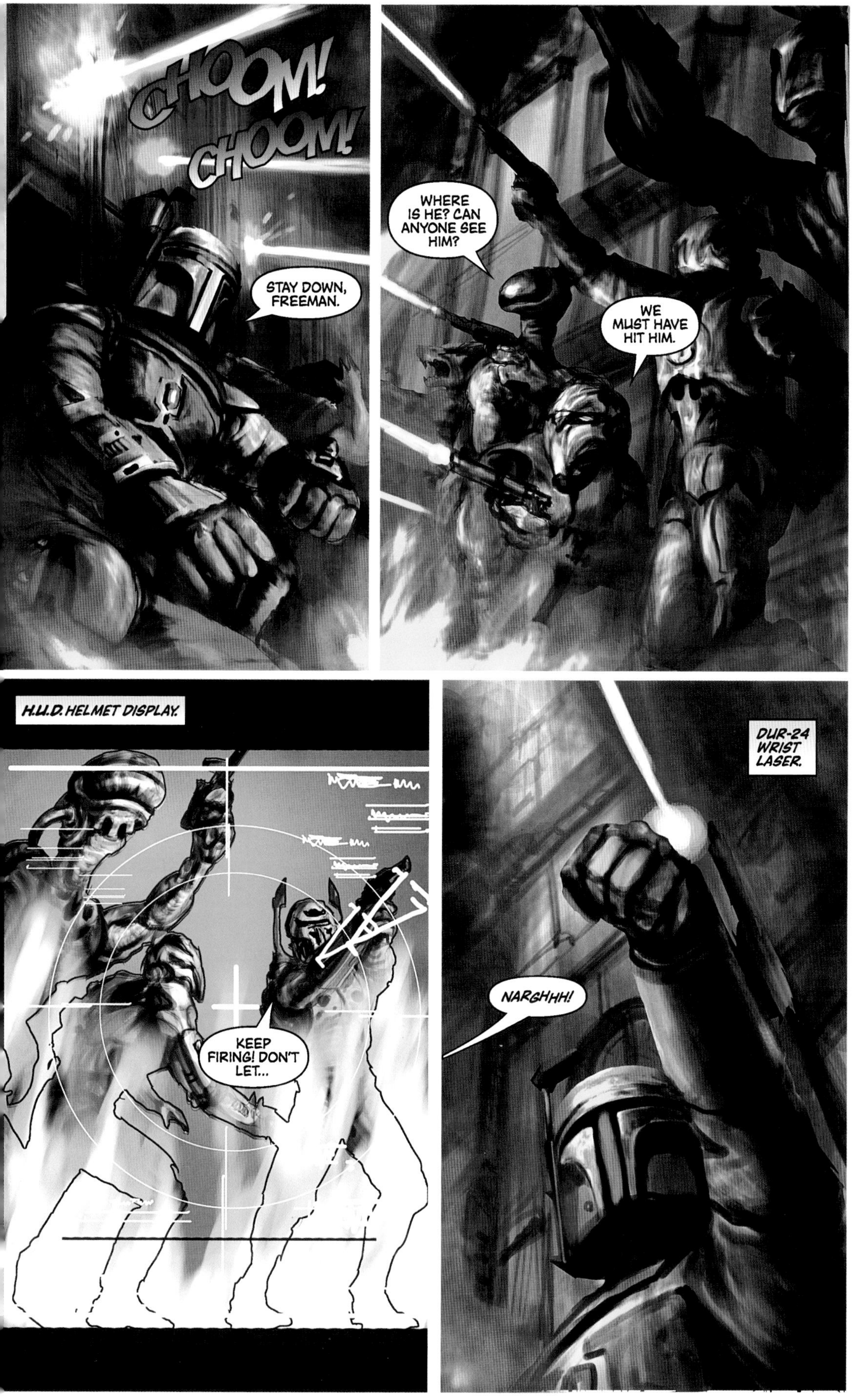
CHOOM! CHOOM!
STAY DOWN, FREEMAN.
WHERE IS HE? CAN ANYONE SEE HIM?
WE MUST HAVE HIT HIM.
H.U.D. HELMET DISPLAY.
KEEP FIRING! DON'T LET...
DUR-24 WRIST LASER.
NARGHHH!

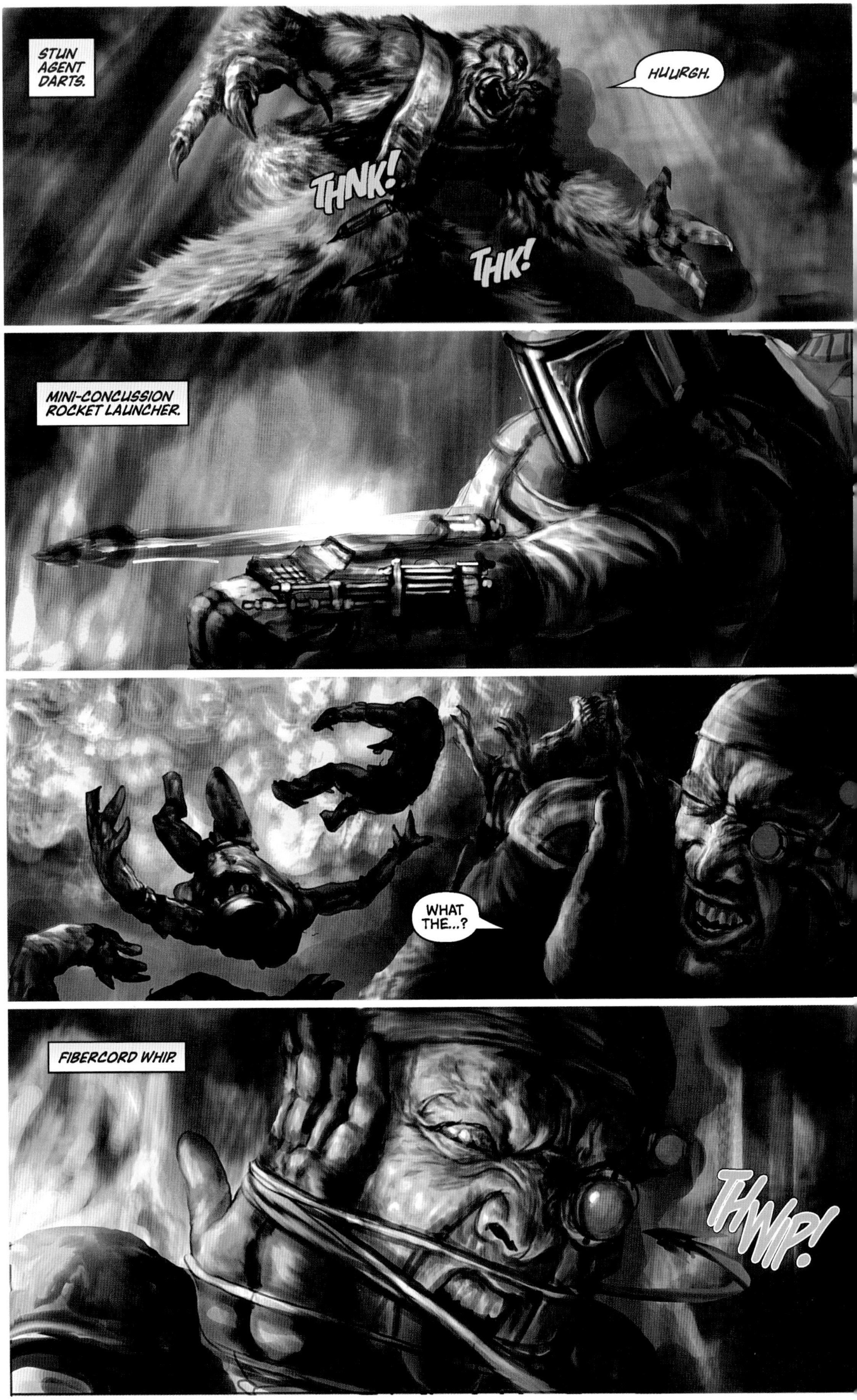
STUN AGENT DARTS.
HUURGH.
THNK!
THK!
MINI-CONCUSSION ROCKET LAUNCHER.
WHAT THE...?
FIBERCORD WHIP.
THWIP!

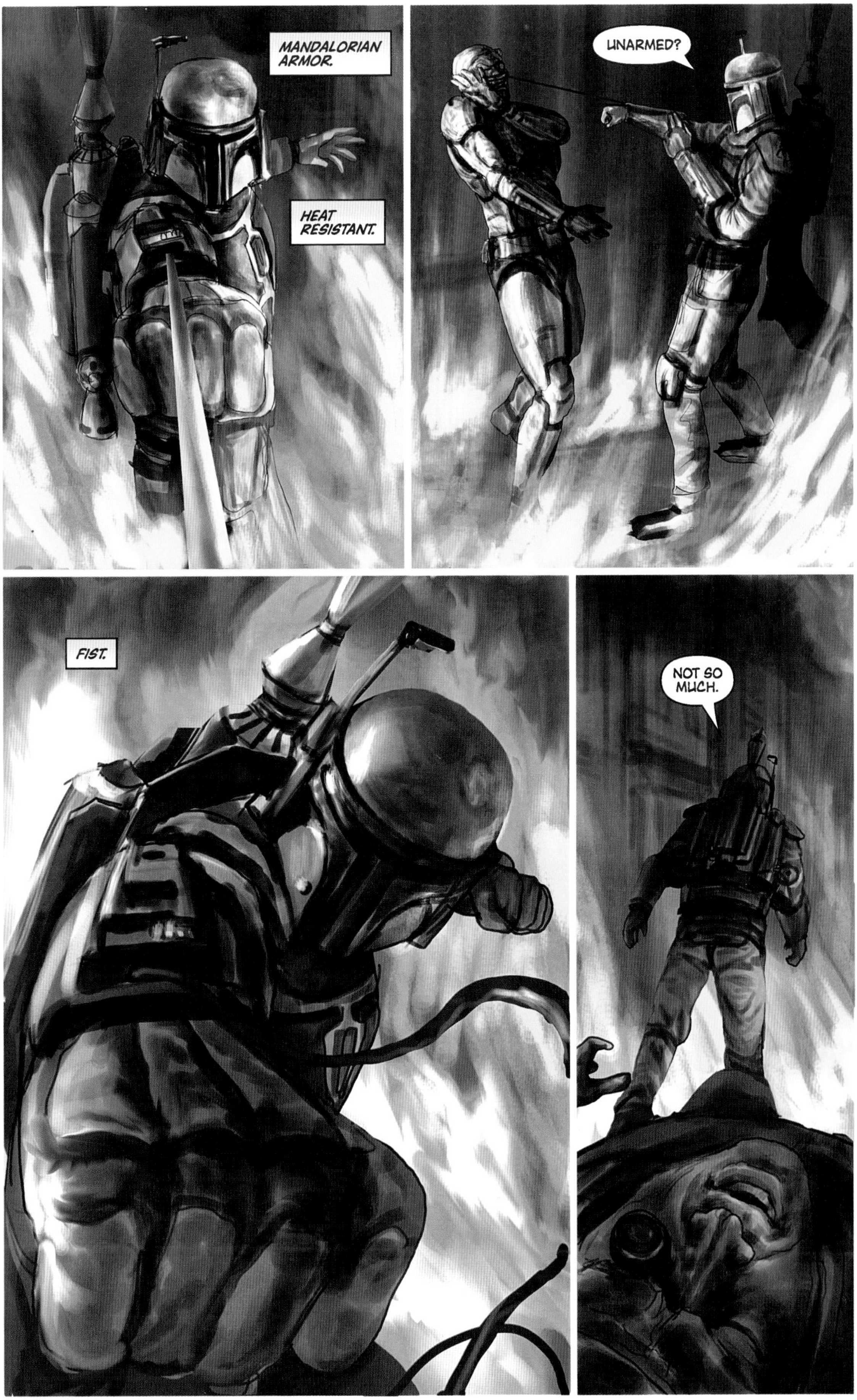
MANDALORIAN ARMOR.
HEAT RESISTANT.
UNARMED?
FIST.
NOT SO MUCH.

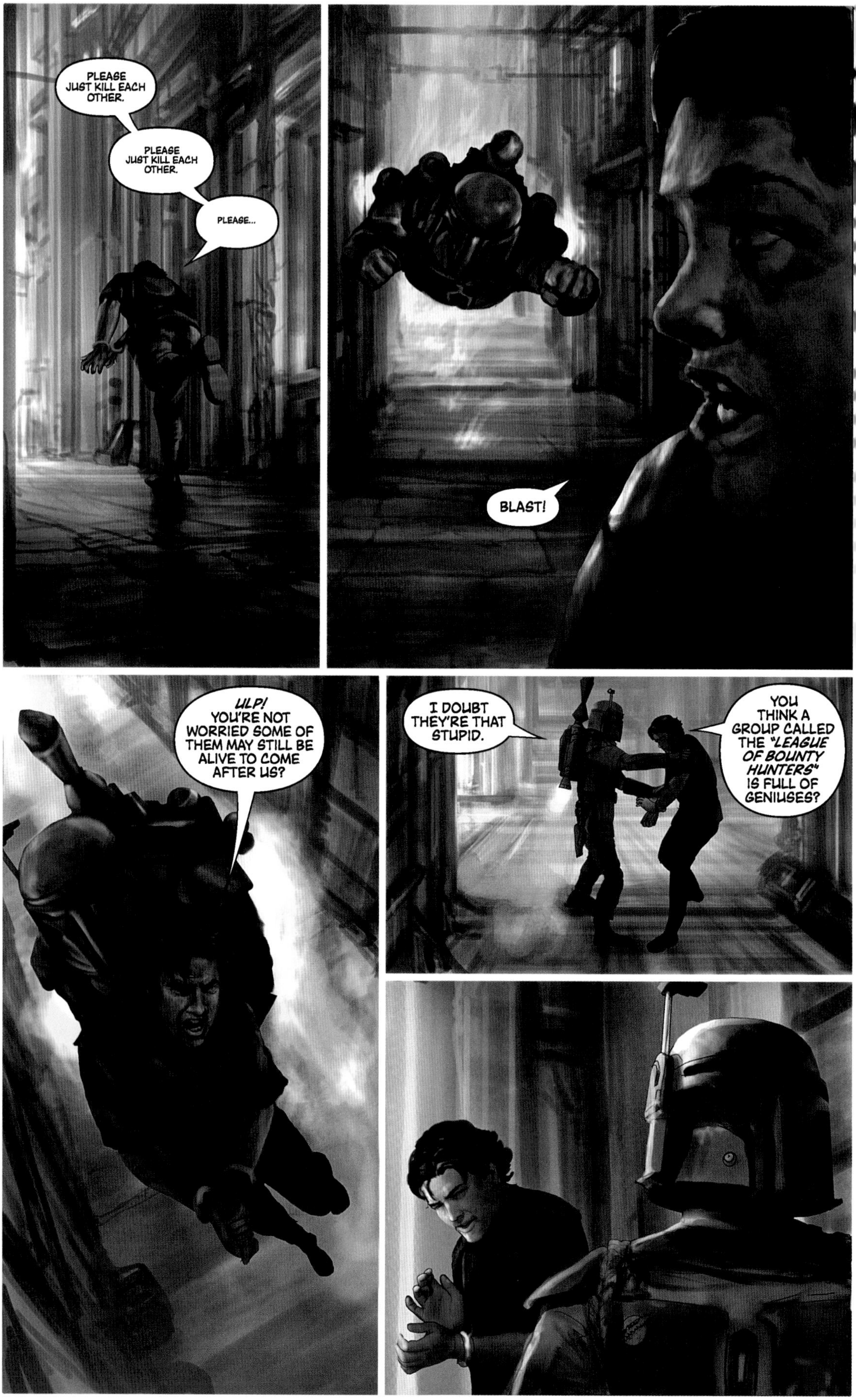
PLEASE JUST KILL EACH OTHER.
PLEASE JUST KILL EACH OTHER.
PLEASE...
BLAST!
ULP! YOU'RE NOT WORRIED SOME OF THEM MAY STILL BE ALIVE TO COME AFTER US?
YOU THINK A GROUP CALLED THE "LEAGUE OF BOUNTY HUNTERS" IS FULL OF GENIUSES?
I DOUBT THEY'RE THAT STUPID.

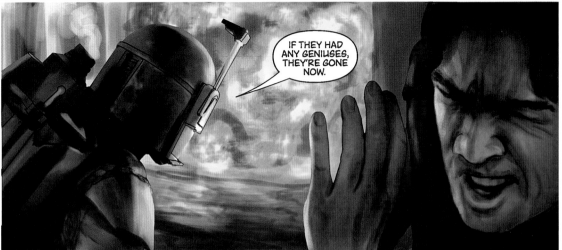

IF THEY HAD ANY GENIUSES, THEY'RE GONE NOW.

NOW --

-- UNCONSCIOUS.

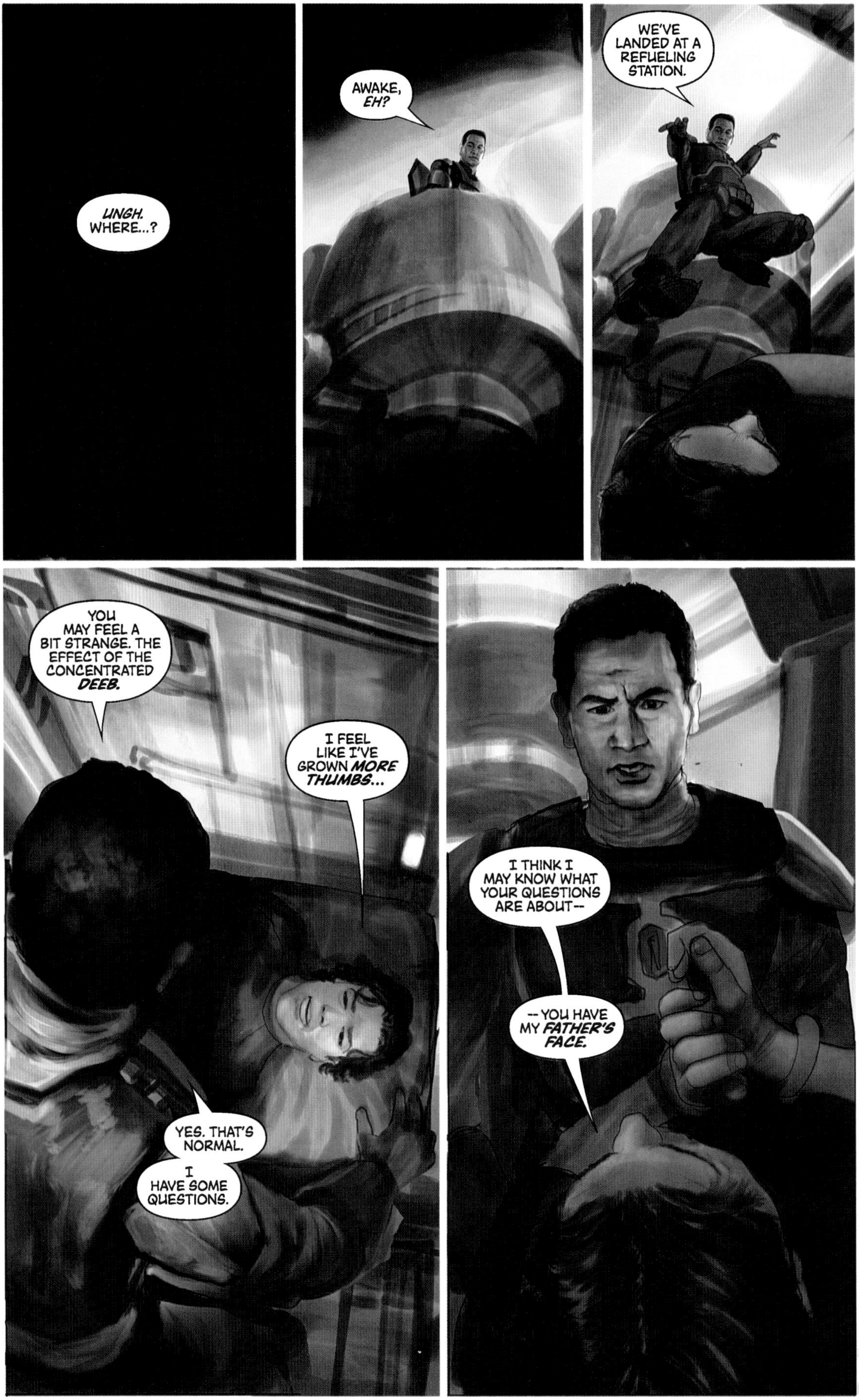
UNGH. WHERE...?
AWAKE, EH?
WE'VE LANDED AT A REFUELING STATION.
YOU MAY FEEL A BIT STRANGE. THE EFFECT OF THE CONCENTRATED DEEB.
I FEEL LIKE I'VE GROWN MORE THUMBS...
YES. THAT'S NORMAL.
I HAVE SOME QUESTIONS.
I THINK I MAY KNOW WHAT YOUR QUESTIONS ARE ABOUT--
--YOU HAVE MY FATHER'S FACE.

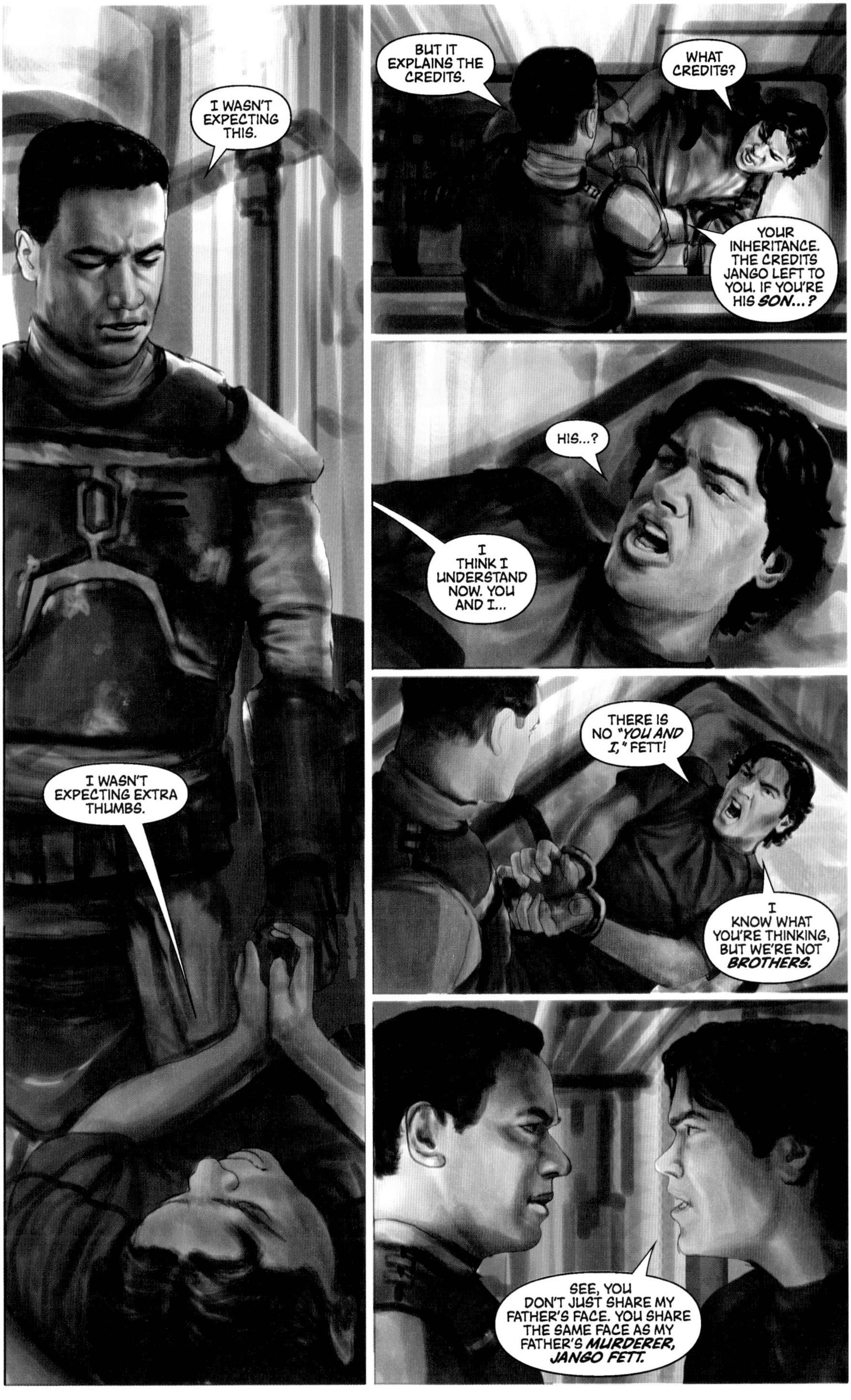
I WASN'T EXPECTING THIS.
I WASN'T EXPECTING EXTRA THUMBS.
BUT IT EXPLAINS THE CREDITS.
WHAT CREDITS?
YOUR INHERITANCE. THE CREDITS JANGO LEFT TO YOU. IF YOU'RE HIS *SON...?*
HIS...?
I THINK I UNDERSTAND NOW. YOU AND I...
THERE IS NO *"YOU AND I,"* FETT!
I KNOW WHAT YOU'RE THINKING, BUT WE'RE NOT *BROTHERS.*
SEE, YOU DON'T JUST SHARE MY FATHER'S FACE. YOU SHARE THE SAME FACE AS MY FATHER'S *MURDERER, JANGO FETT.*

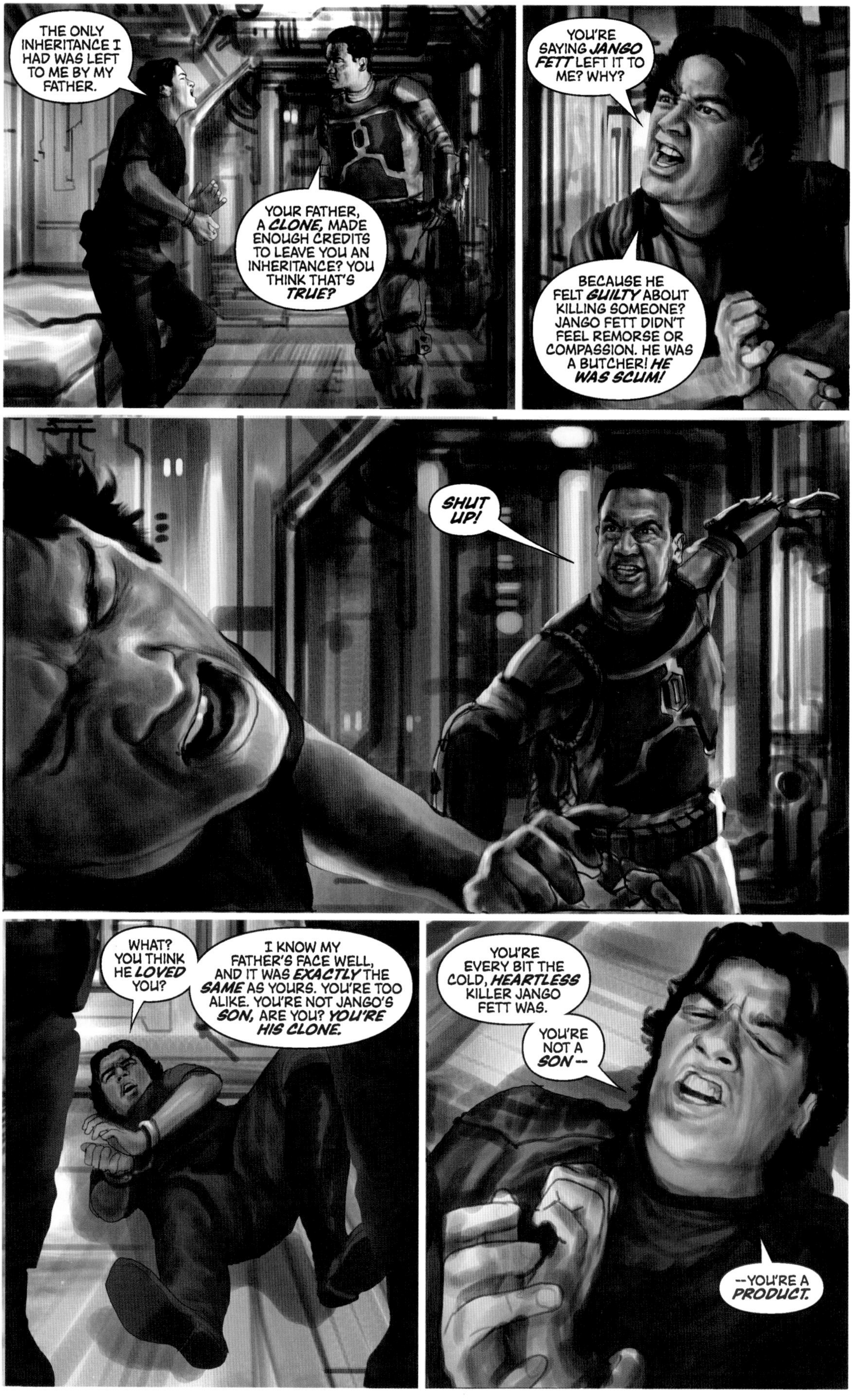
THE ONLY INHERITANCE I HAD WAS LEFT TO ME BY MY FATHER.
YOUR FATHER, A CLONE, MADE ENOUGH CREDITS TO LEAVE YOU AN INHERITANCE? YOU THINK THAT'S TRUE?
YOU'RE SAYING JANGO FETT LEFT IT TO ME? WHY?
BECAUSE HE FELT GUILTY ABOUT KILLING SOMEONE? JANGO FETT DIDN'T FEEL REMORSE OR COMPASSION. HE WAS A BUTCHER! HE WAS SCUM!
SHUT UP!
WHAT? YOU THINK HE LOVED YOU?
I KNOW MY FATHER'S FACE WELL, AND IT WAS EXACTLY THE SAME AS YOURS. YOU'RE TOO ALIKE. YOU'RE NOT JANGO'S SON, ARE YOU? YOU'RE HIS CLONE.
YOU'RE EVERY BIT THE COLD, HEARTLESS KILLER JANGO FETT WAS.
YOU'RE NOT A SON--
--YOU'RE A PRODUCT.

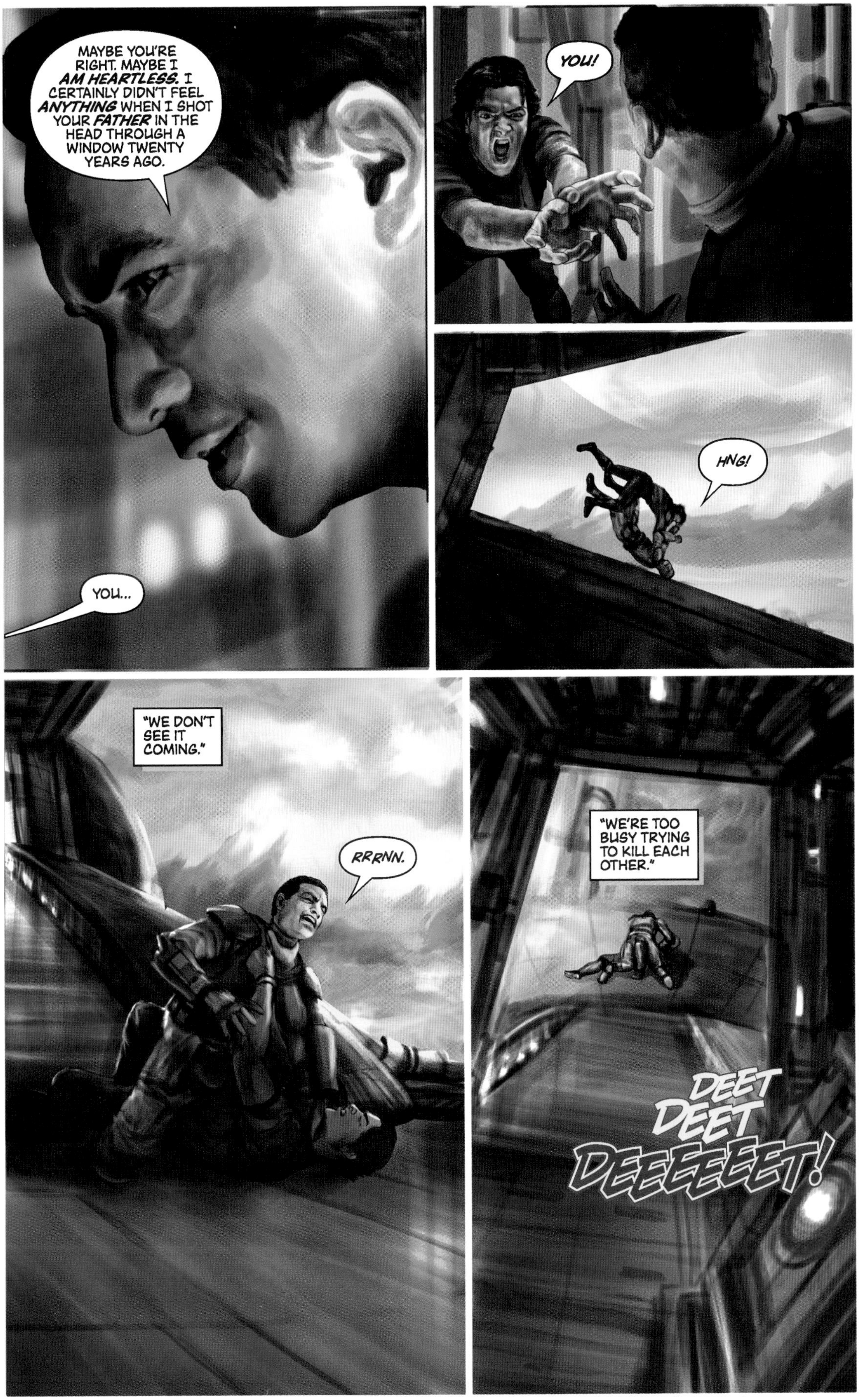
MAYBE YOU'RE RIGHT. MAYBE I AM HEARTLESS. I CERTAINLY DIDN'T FEEL ANYTHING WHEN I SHOT YOUR FATHER IN THE HEAD THROUGH A WINDOW TWENTY YEARS AGO.
YOU...
YOU!
HNG!
"WE DON'T SEE IT COMING."
RRRNN.
"WE'RE TOO BUSY TRYING TO KILL EACH OTHER."
DEET DEET DEEEEEEET!

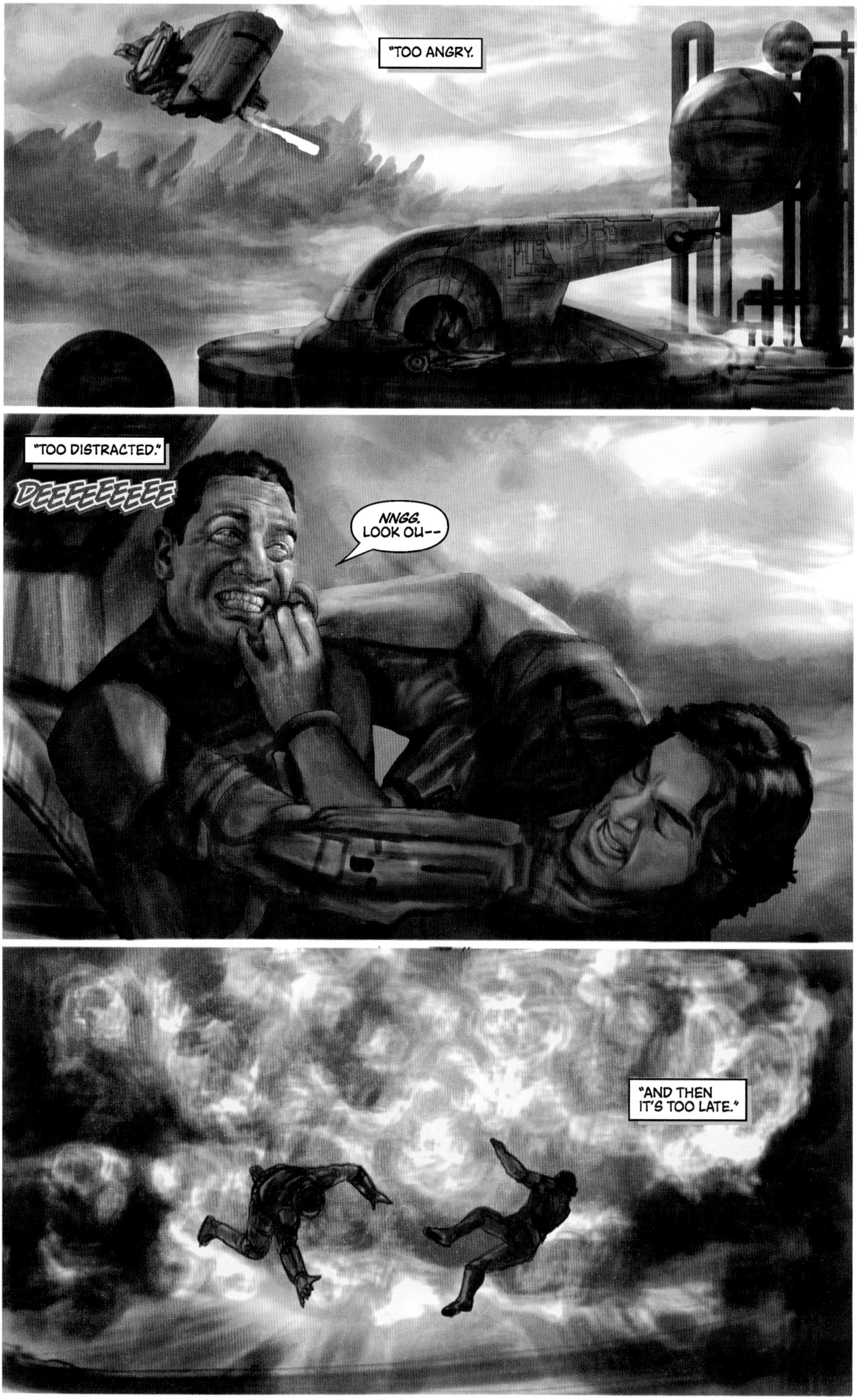
"TOO ANGRY.
"TOO DISTRACTED."
DEEEEEEEEE
NNGG.
LOOK OU--
"AND THEN
IT'S TOO LATE."

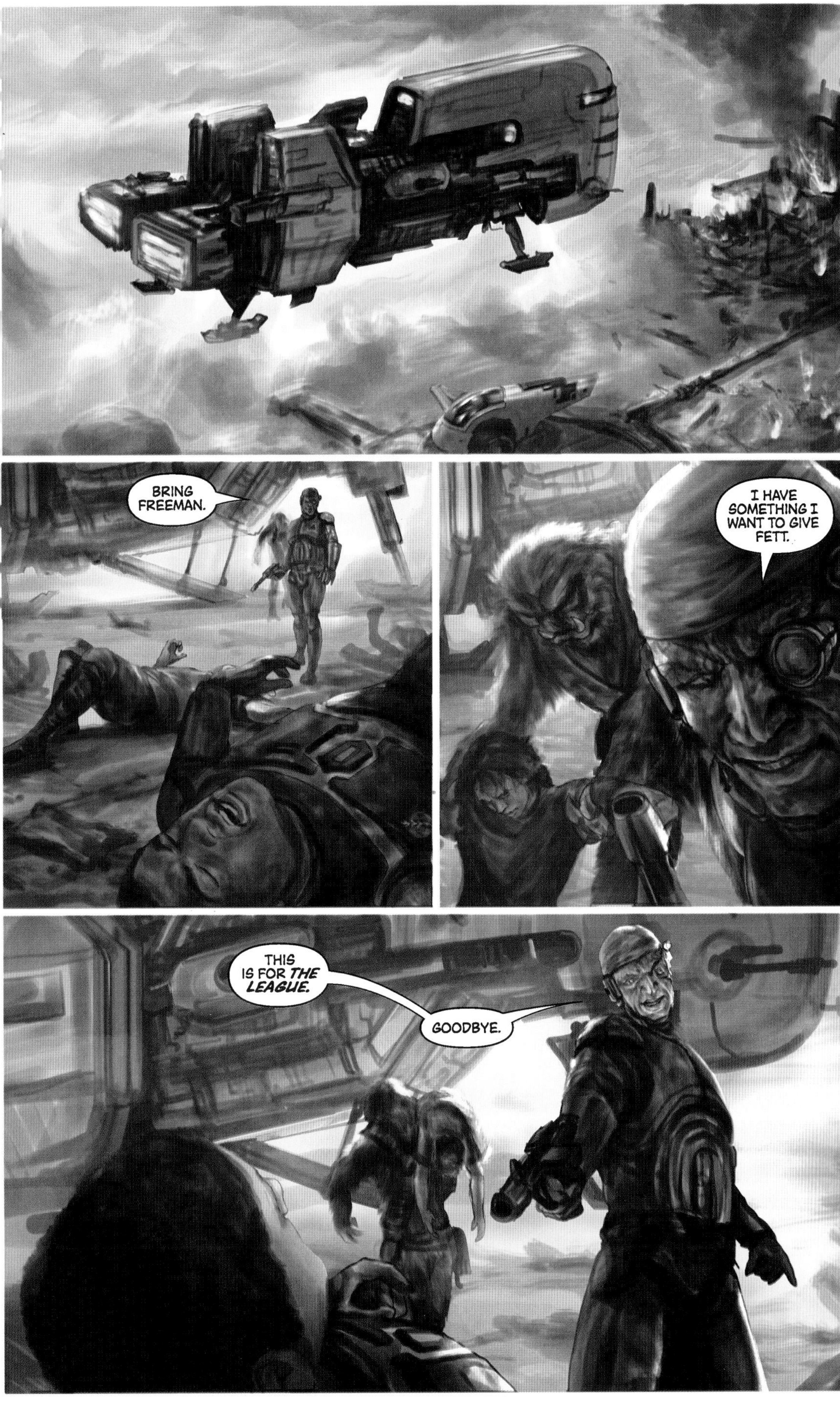
BRING FREEMAN.
I HAVE SOMETHING I WANT TO GIVE FETT.
THIS IS FOR *THE LEAGUE.*
GOODBYE.

HNNN... BYE.

?

WHAT'S THE MATTER? CAN'T SHOOT A *DEFENSELESS MAN* IN THE *FACE?*

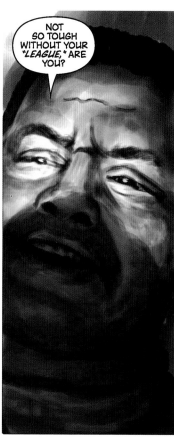

NOT SO TOUGH WITHOUT YOUR *"LEAGUE,"* ARE YOU?

CHOOM!

CHOOM!

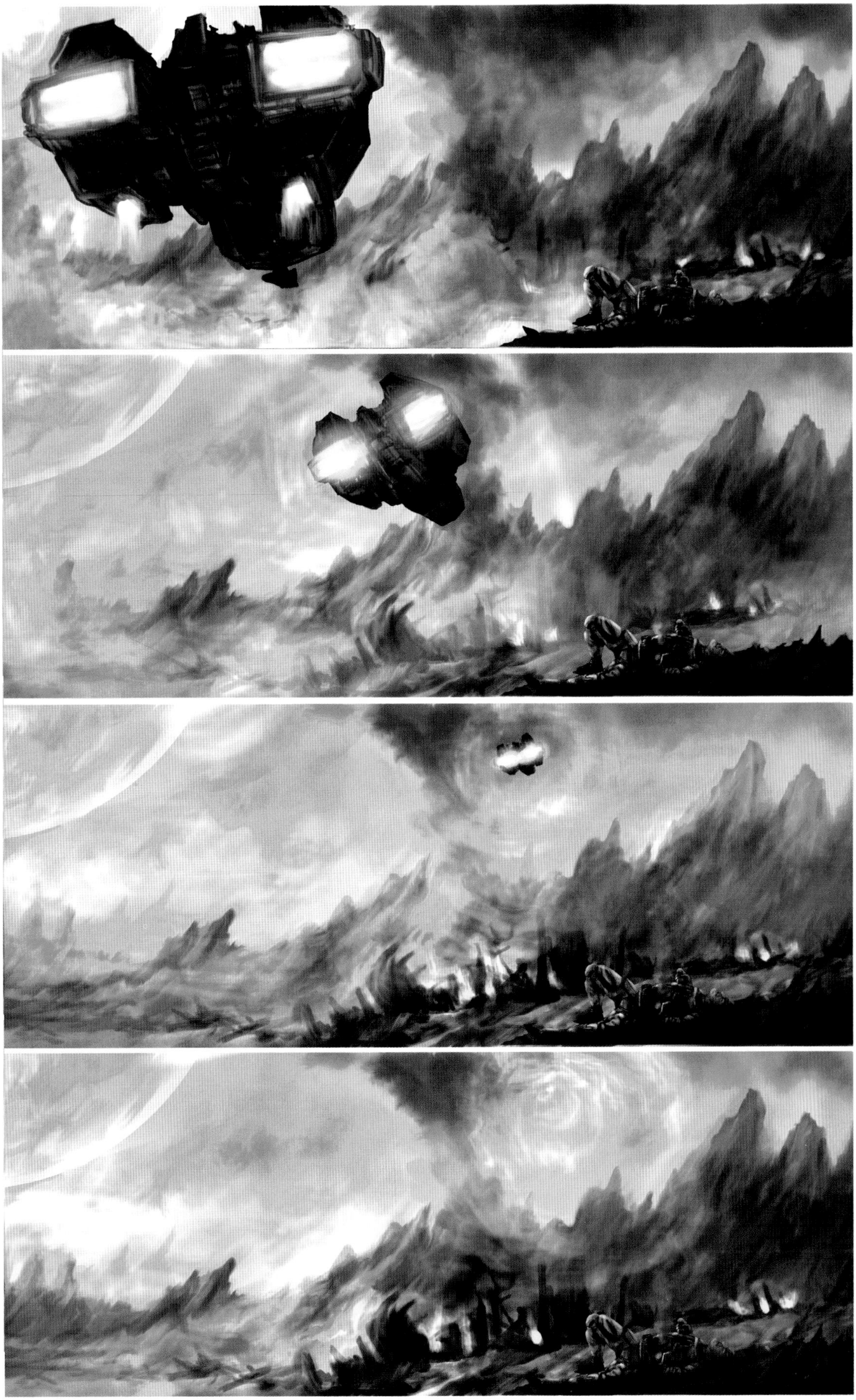

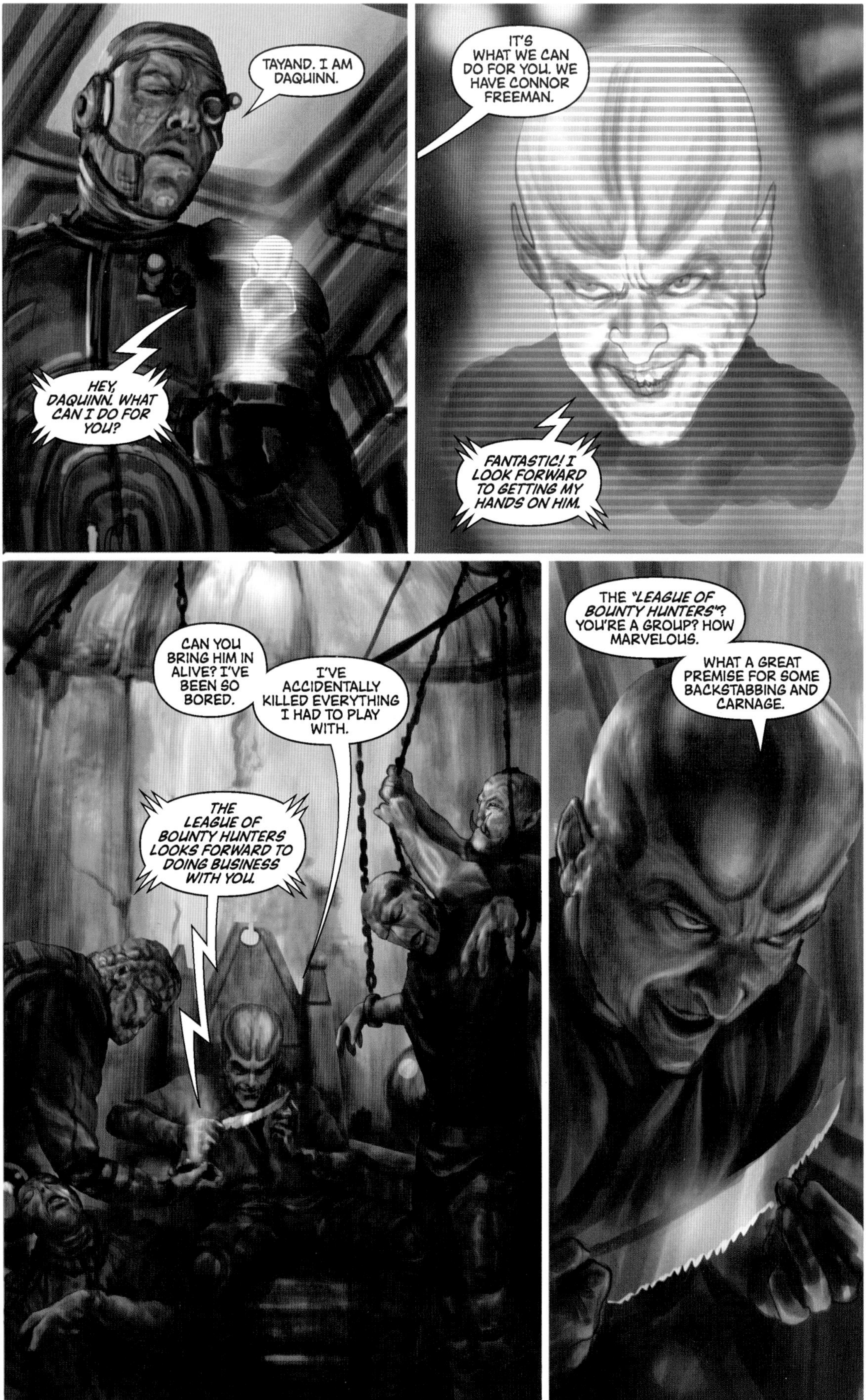
TAYAND. I AM DAQUINN.
HEY, DAQUINN. WHAT CAN I DO FOR YOU?
IT'S WHAT WE CAN DO FOR YOU. WE HAVE CONNOR FREEMAN.
FANTASTIC! I LOOK FORWARD TO GETTING MY HANDS ON HIM.
CAN YOU BRING HIM IN ALIVE? I'VE BEEN SO BORED.
I'VE ACCIDENTALLY KILLED EVERYTHING I HAD TO PLAY WITH.
THE LEAGUE OF BOUNTY HUNTERS LOOKS FORWARD TO DOING BUSINESS WITH YOU.
THE "LEAGUE OF BOUNTY HUNTERS"? YOU'RE A GROUP? HOW MARVELOUS.
WHAT A GREAT PREMISE FOR SOME BACKSTABBING AND CARNAGE.

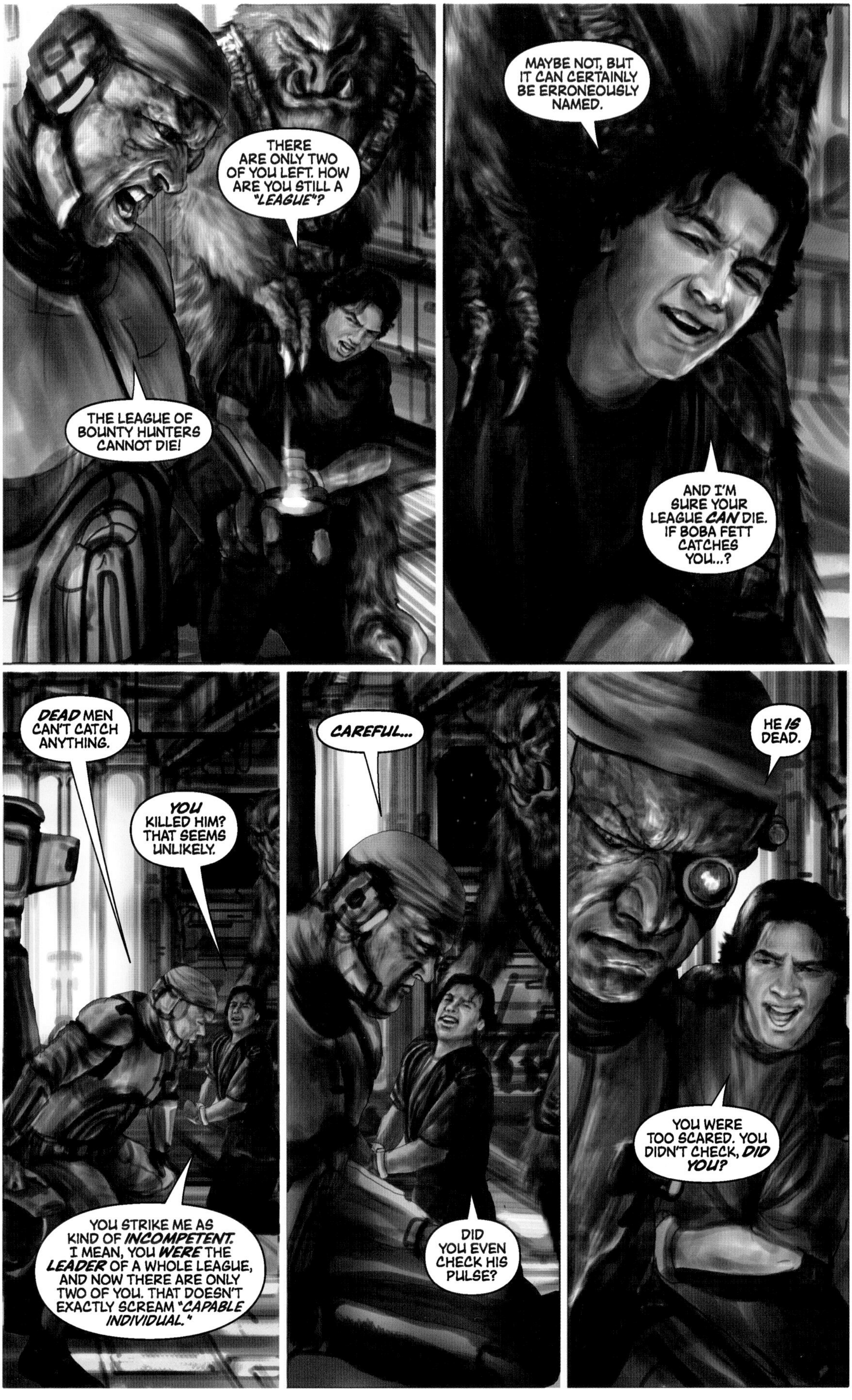
THERE ARE ONLY TWO OF YOU LEFT. HOW ARE YOU STILL A "LEAGUE"?
THE LEAGUE OF BOUNTY HUNTERS CANNOT DIE!
MAYBE NOT, BUT IT CAN CERTAINLY BE ERRONEOUSLY NAMED.
AND I'M SURE YOUR LEAGUE CAN DIE. IF BOBA FETT CATCHES YOU...?
DEAD MEN CAN'T CATCH ANYTHING.
YOU KILLED HIM? THAT SEEMS UNLIKELY.
YOU STRIKE ME AS KIND OF INCOMPETENT. I MEAN, YOU WERE THE LEADER OF A WHOLE LEAGUE, AND NOW THERE ARE ONLY TWO OF YOU. THAT DOESN'T EXACTLY SCREAM "CAPABLE INDIVIDUAL."
CAREFUL...
DID YOU EVEN CHECK HIS PULSE?
HE IS DEAD.
YOU WERE TOO SCARED. YOU DIDN'T CHECK, DID YOU?

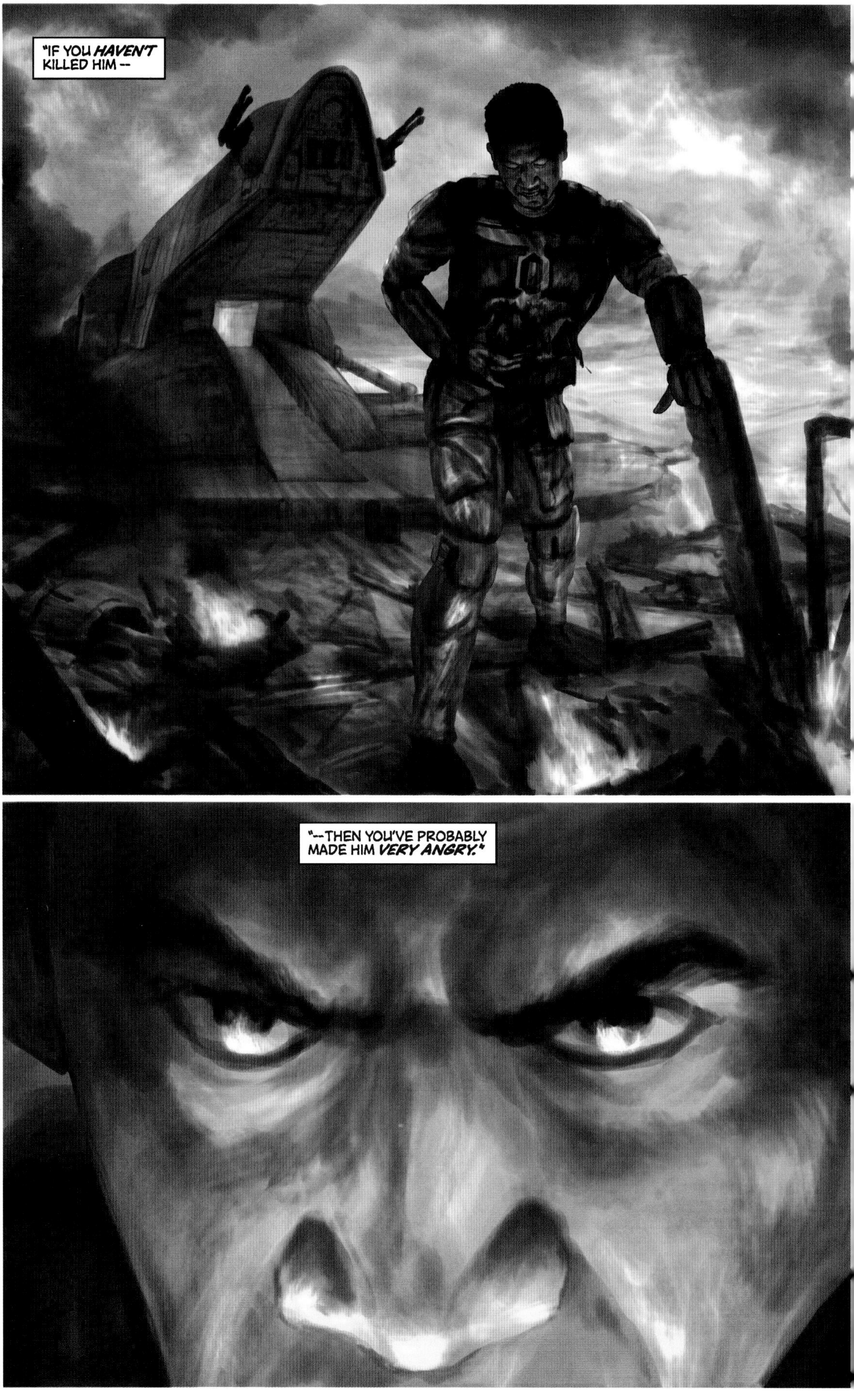
"IF YOU *HAVEN'T* KILLED HIM --
"--THEN YOU'VE PROBABLY MADE HIM *VERY ANGRY.*"

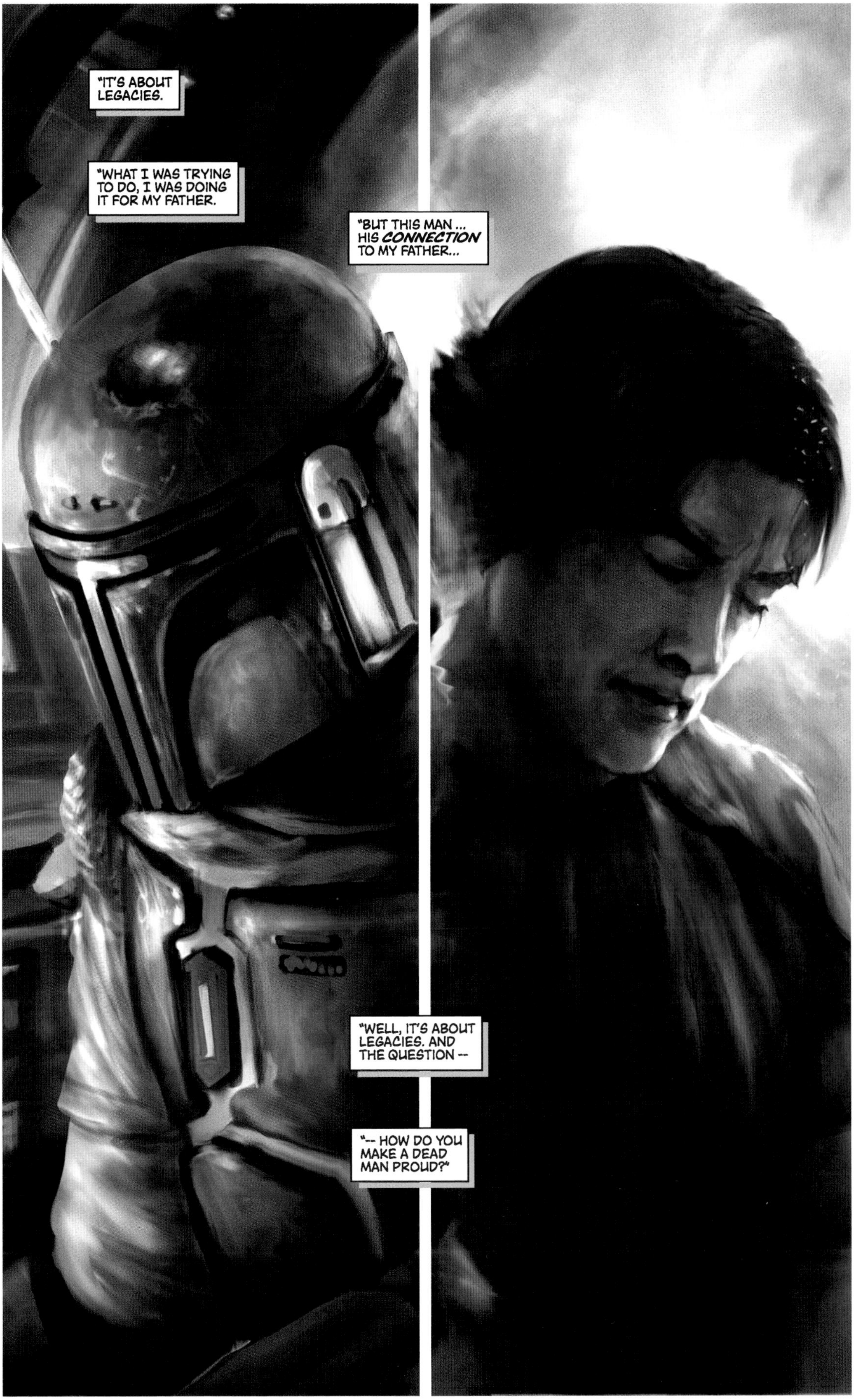
"IT'S ABOUT LEGACIES.
"WHAT I WAS TRYING TO DO, I WAS DOING IT FOR MY FATHER.
"BUT THIS MAN ... HIS *CONNECTION* TO MY FATHER...
"WELL, IT'S ABOUT LEGACIES. AND THE QUESTION --
"-- HOW DO YOU MAKE A DEAD MAN PROUD?"

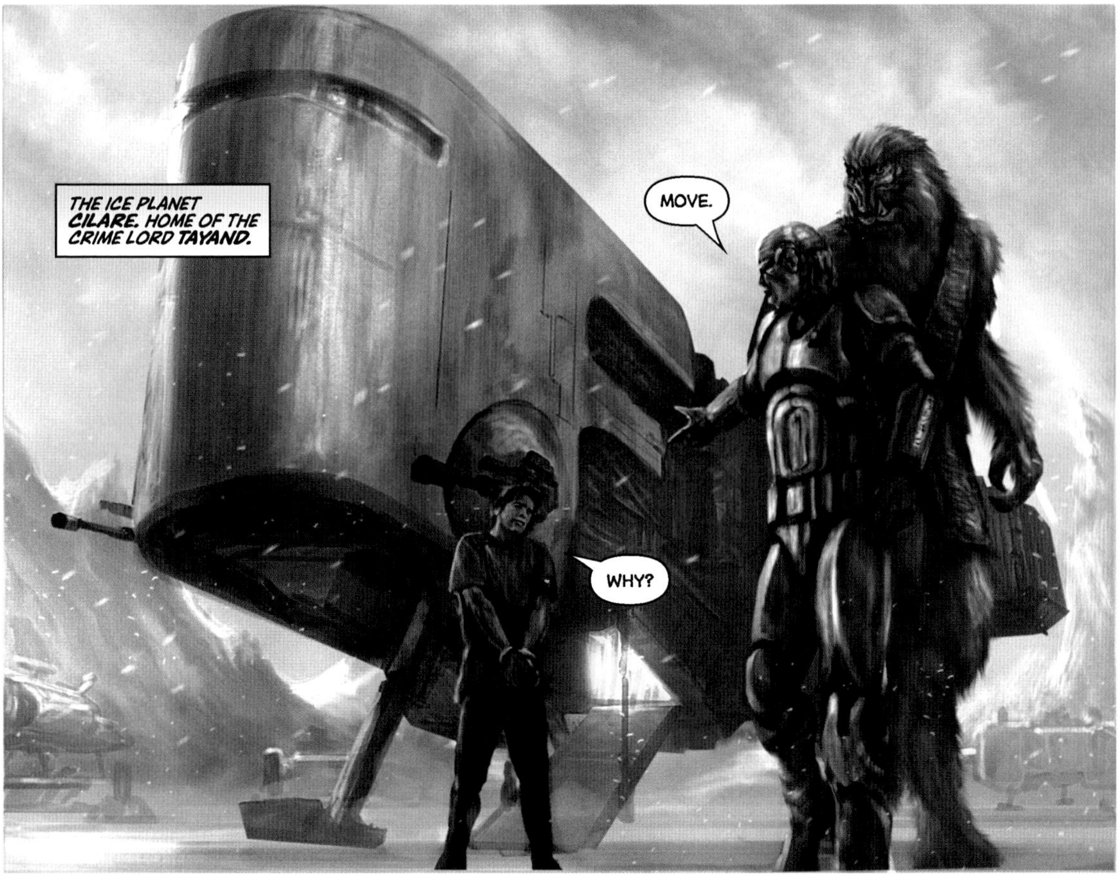
THE ICE PLANET CILARE. HOME OF THE CRIME LORD TAYAND.
MOVE.
WHY?

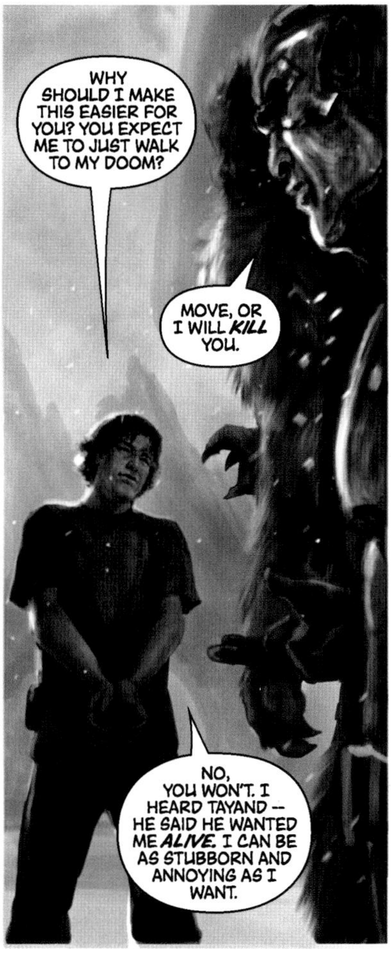
WHY SHOULD I MAKE THIS EASIER FOR YOU? YOU EXPECT ME TO JUST WALK TO MY DOOM?
MOVE, OR I WILL KILL YOU.
NO, YOU WON'T. I HEARD TAYAND -- HE SAID HE WANTED ME ALIVE. I CAN BE AS STUBBORN AND ANNOYING AS I WANT.

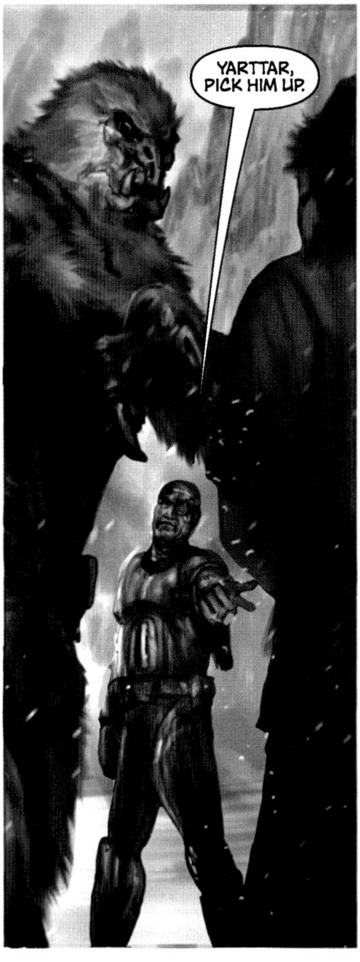
YARTTAR, PICK HIM UP.

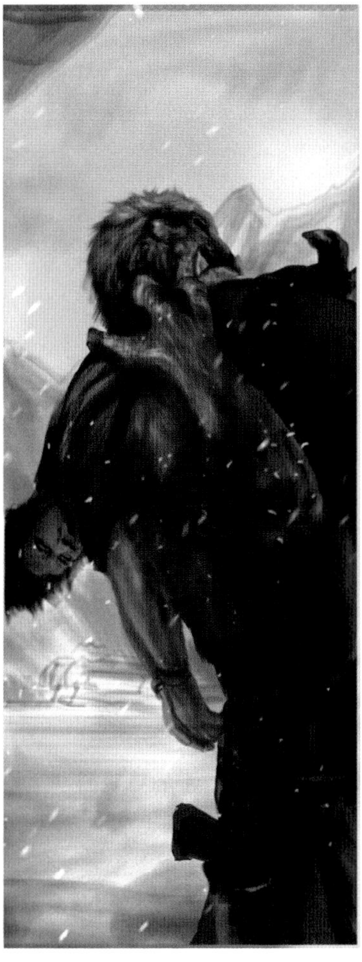

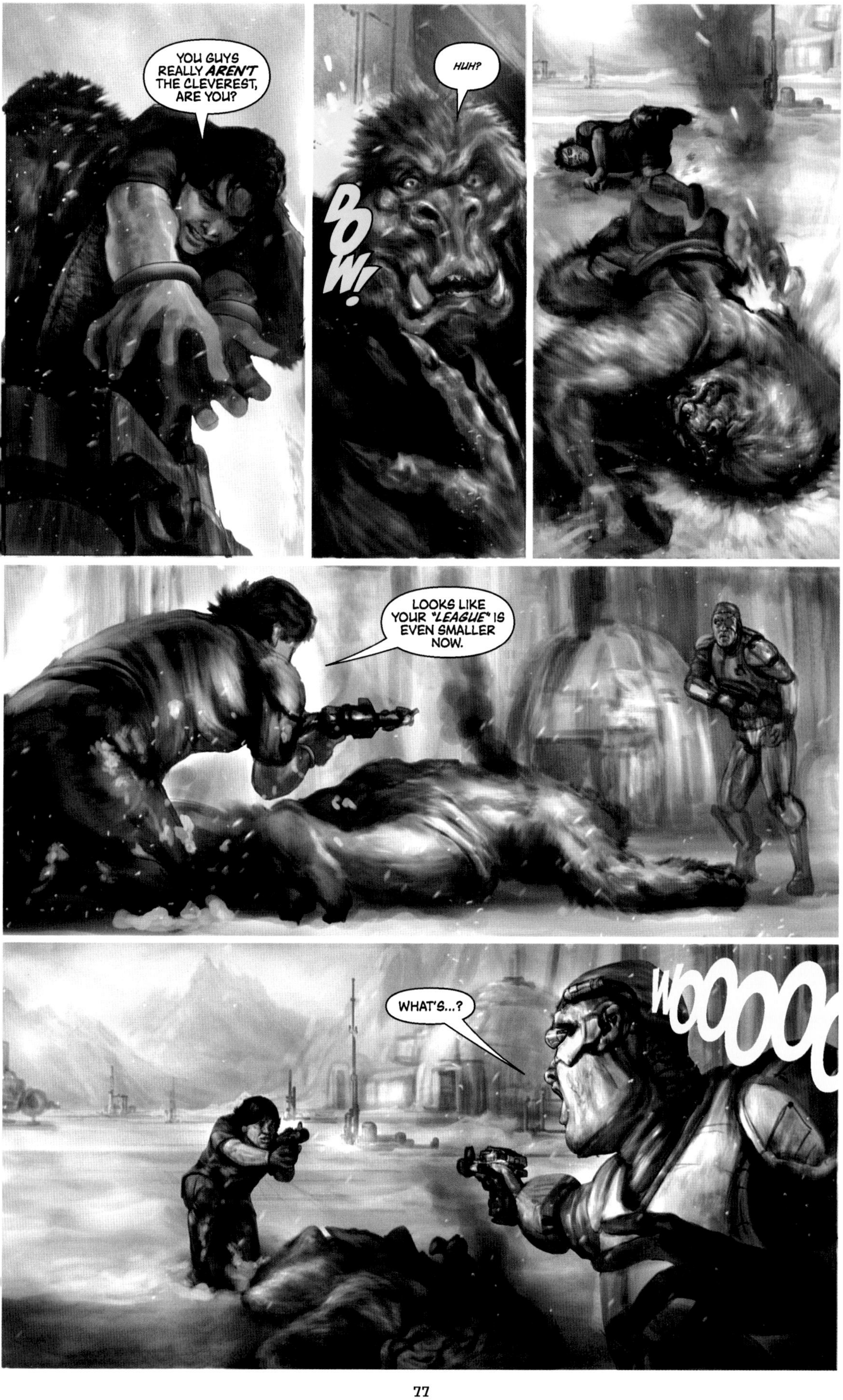
YOU GUYS REALLY *AREN'T* THE CLEVEREST, ARE YOU?
HUH?
DOOW!
LOOKS LIKE YOUR *"LEAGUE"* IS EVEN SMALLER NOW.
WHAT'S...?
WOOOO

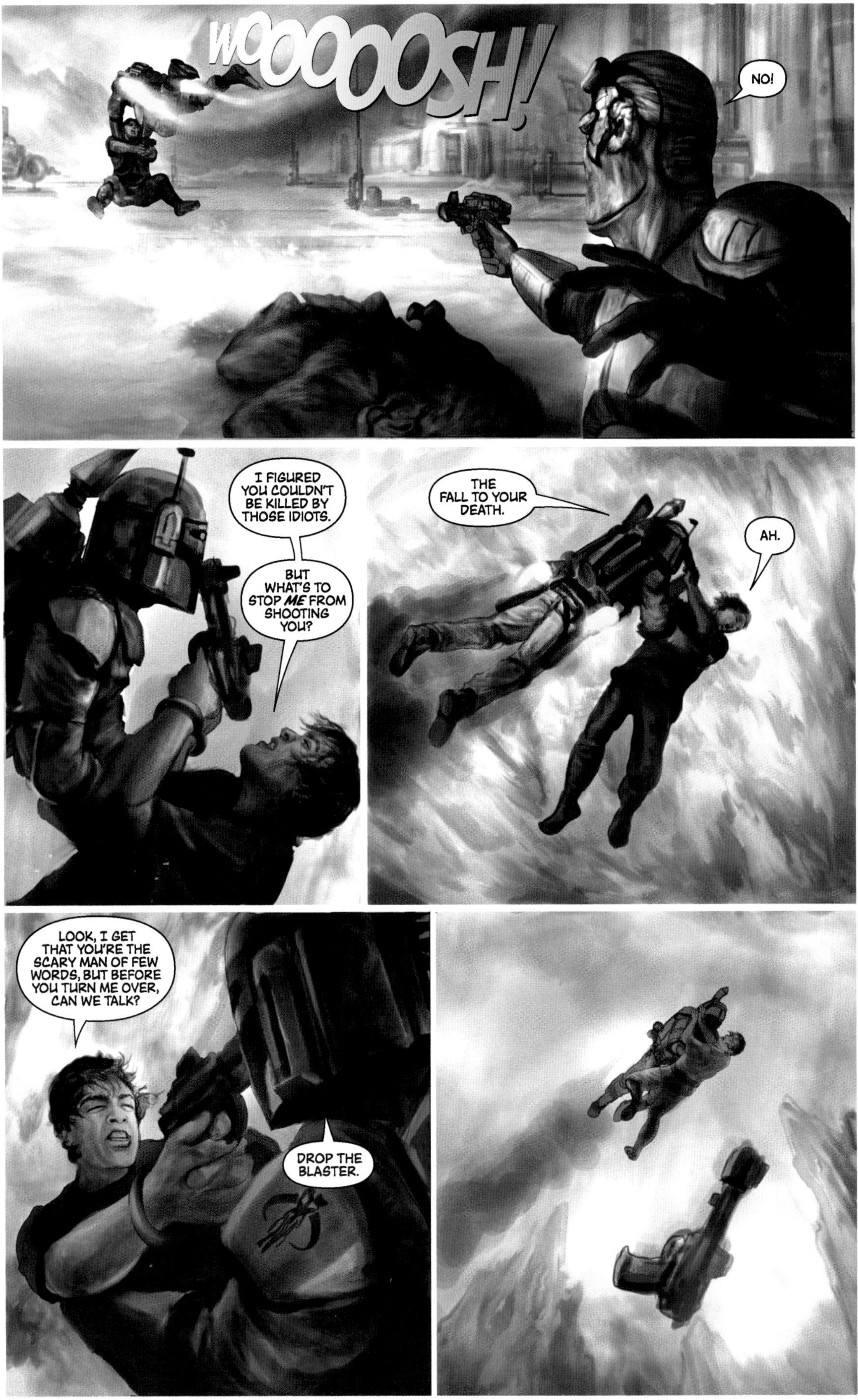
WOOOOOOSH!
NO!
I FIGURED YOU COULDN'T BE KILLED BY THOSE IDIOTS.
BUT WHAT'S TO STOP *ME* FROM SHOOTING YOU?
THE FALL TO YOUR DEATH.
AH.
LOOK, I GET THAT YOU'RE THE SCARY MAN OF FEW WORDS, BUT BEFORE YOU TURN ME OVER, CAN WE TALK?
DROP THE BLASTER.

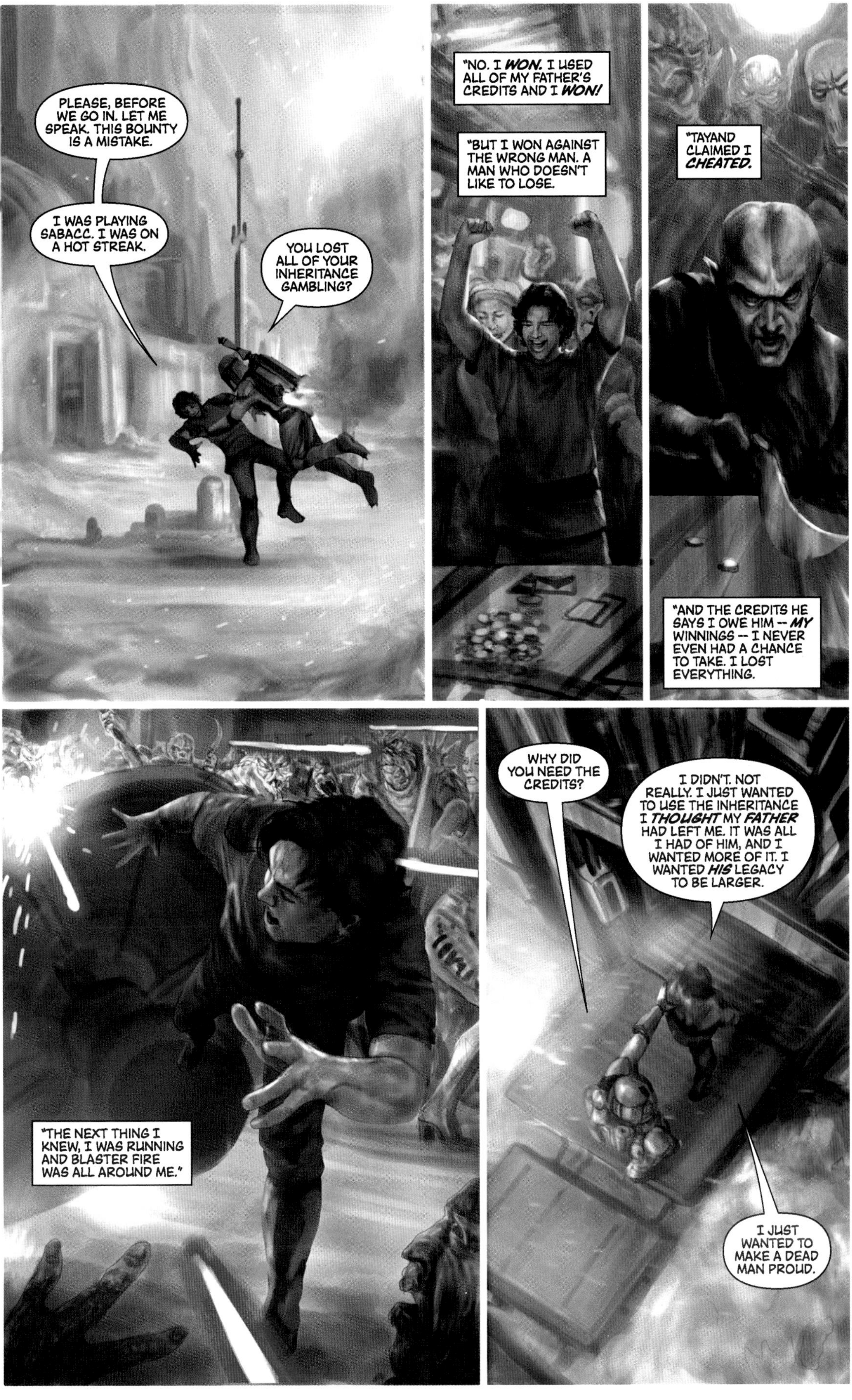
PLEASE, BEFORE WE GO IN. LET ME SPEAK. THIS BOUNTY IS A MISTAKE.
I WAS PLAYING SABACC. I WAS ON A HOT STREAK.
YOU LOST ALL OF YOUR INHERITANCE GAMBLING?
"NO. I *WON.* I USED ALL OF MY FATHER'S CREDITS AND I *WON!*
"BUT I WON AGAINST THE WRONG MAN. A MAN WHO DOESN'T LIKE TO LOSE.
"TAYAND CLAIMED I *CHEATED.*
"AND THE CREDITS HE SAYS I OWE HIM -- *MY* WINNINGS -- I NEVER EVEN HAD A CHANCE TO TAKE. I LOST EVERYTHING.
"THE NEXT THING I KNEW, I WAS RUNNING AND BLASTER FIRE WAS ALL AROUND ME."
WHY DID YOU NEED THE CREDITS?
I DIDN'T. NOT REALLY. I JUST WANTED TO USE THE INHERITANCE I *THOUGHT* MY *FATHER* HAD LEFT ME. IT WAS ALL I HAD OF HIM, AND I WANTED MORE OF IT. I WANTED *HIS* LEGACY TO BE LARGER.
I JUST WANTED TO MAKE A DEAD MAN PROUD.

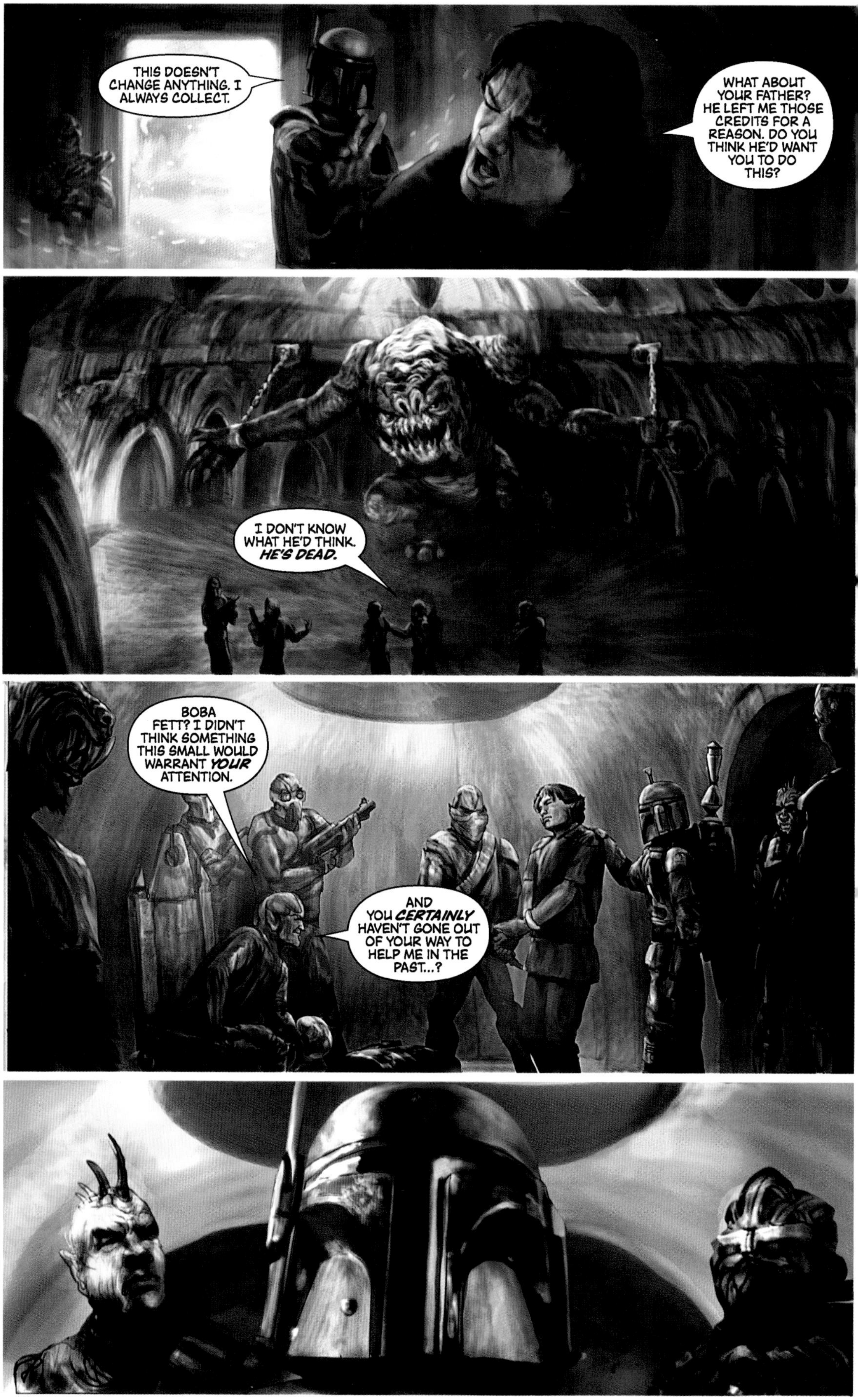
THIS DOESN'T CHANGE ANYTHING. I ALWAYS COLLECT.
WHAT ABOUT YOUR FATHER? HE LEFT ME THOSE CREDITS FOR A REASON. DO YOU THINK HE'D WANT YOU TO DO THIS?
I DON'T KNOW WHAT HE'D THINK. HE'S DEAD.
BOBA FETT? I DIDN'T THINK SOMETHING THIS SMALL WOULD WARRANT YOUR ATTENTION.
AND YOU CERTAINLY HAVEN'T GONE OUT OF YOUR WAY TO HELP ME IN THE PAST...?

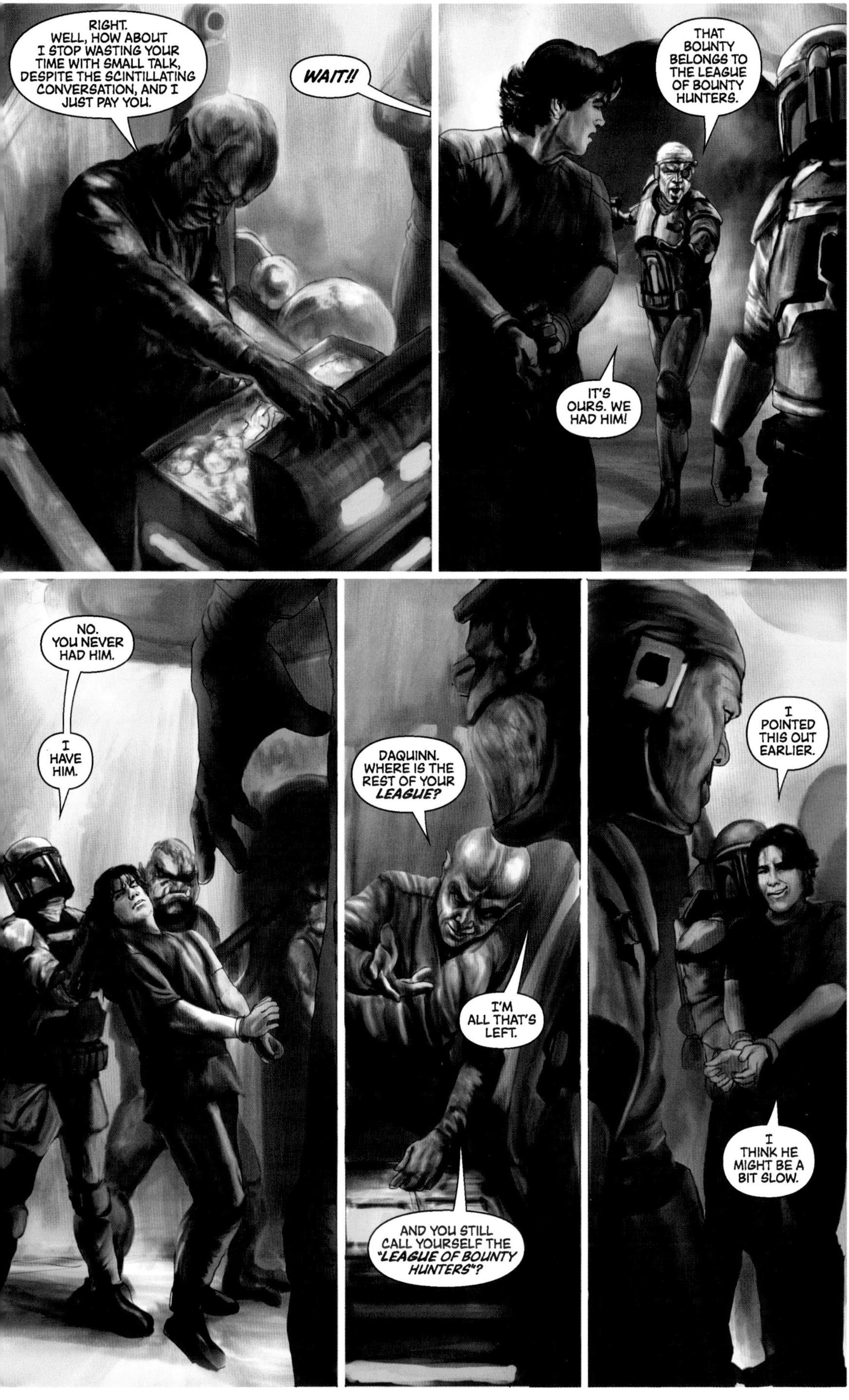
RIGHT. WELL, HOW ABOUT I STOP WASTING YOUR TIME WITH SMALL TALK, DESPITE THE SCINTILLATING CONVERSATION, AND I JUST PAY YOU.
WAIT!!
THAT BOUNTY BELONGS TO THE LEAGUE OF BOUNTY HUNTERS.
IT'S OURS. WE HAD HIM!
NO. YOU NEVER HAD HIM.
I HAVE HIM.
DAQUINN. WHERE IS THE REST OF YOUR *LEAGUE?*
I'M ALL THAT'S LEFT.
AND YOU STILL CALL YOURSELF THE *"LEAGUE OF BOUNTY HUNTERS"*?
I POINTED THIS OUT EARLIER.
I THINK HE MIGHT BE A BIT SLOW.

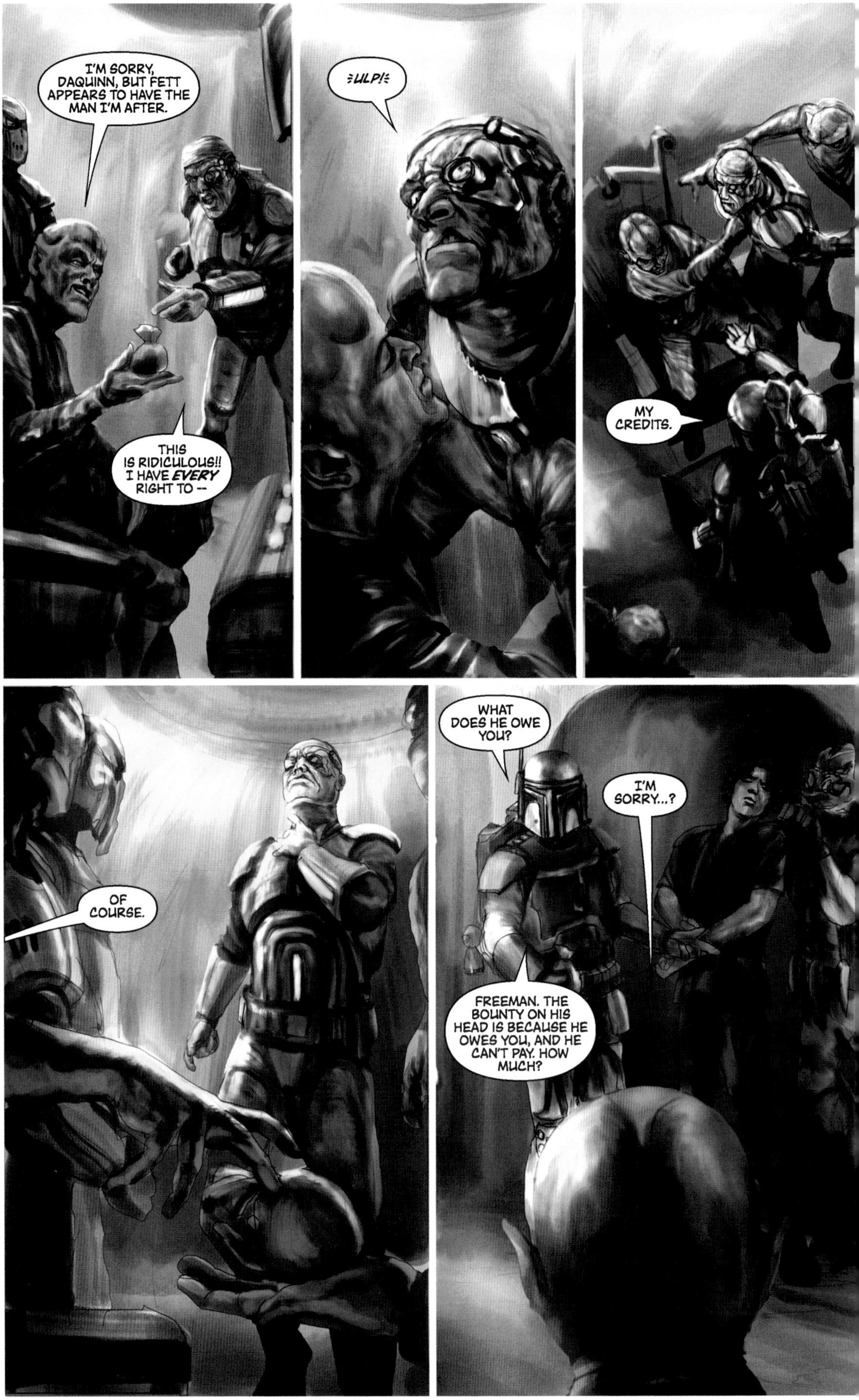

I'M SORRY, DAQUINN, BUT FETT APPEARS TO HAVE THE MAN I'M AFTER.
THIS IS RIDICULOUS!! I HAVE *EVERY* RIGHT TO --
ULP!
MY CREDITS.
OF COURSE.
WHAT DOES HE OWE YOU?
I'M SORRY...?
FREEMAN. THE BOUNTY ON HIS HEAD IS BECAUSE HE OWES YOU, AND HE CAN'T PAY. HOW MUCH?

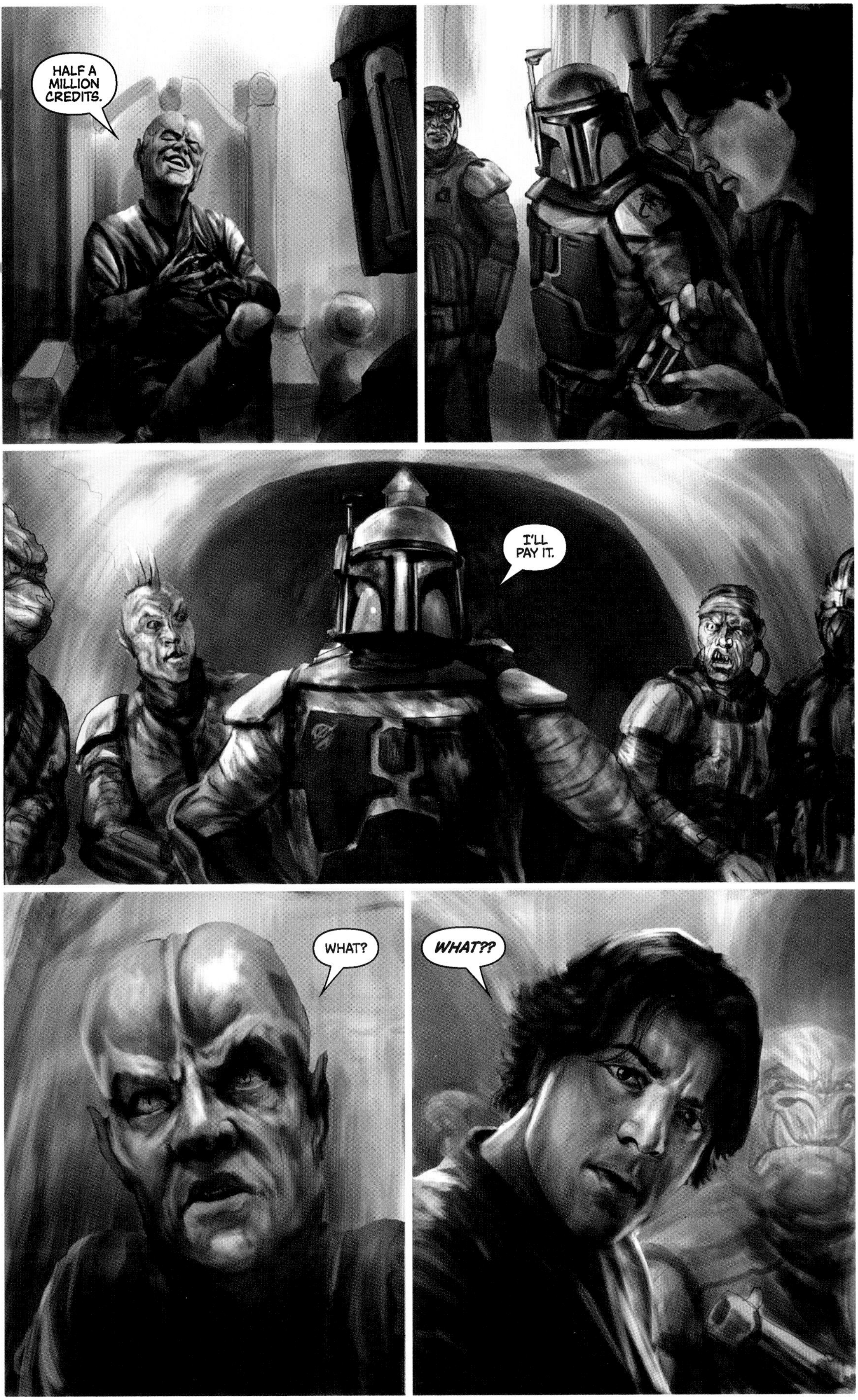
HALF A MILLION CREDITS.
I'LL PAY IT.
WHAT?
WHAT??

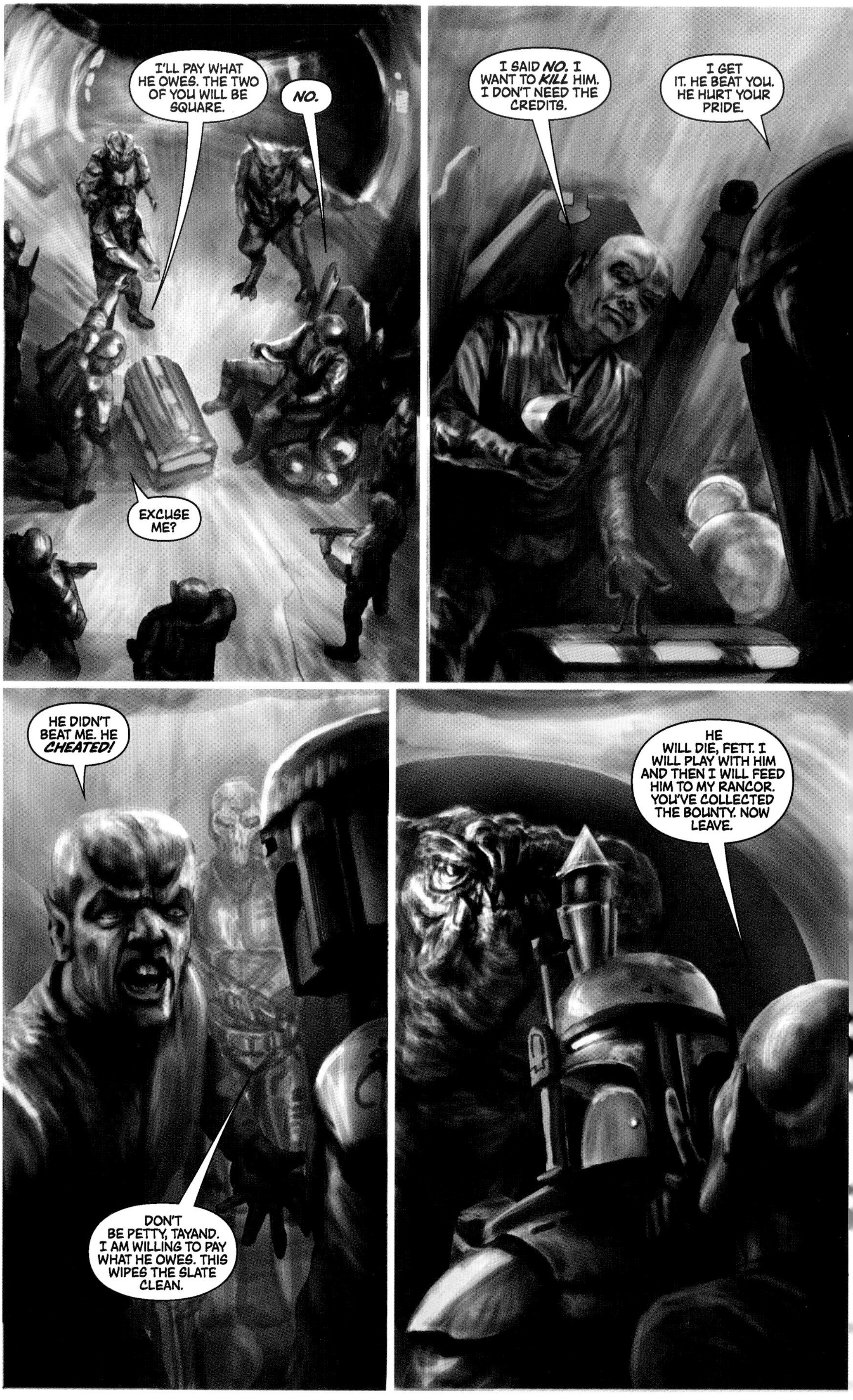
I'LL PAY WHAT HE OWES. THE TWO OF YOU WILL BE SQUARE.
NO.
EXCUSE ME?
I SAID NO. I WANT TO KILL HIM. I DON'T NEED THE CREDITS.
I GET IT. HE BEAT YOU. HE HURT YOUR PRIDE.
HE DIDN'T BEAT ME. HE CHEATED!
DON'T BE PETTY, TAYAND. I AM WILLING TO PAY WHAT HE OWES. THIS WIPES THE SLATE CLEAN.
HE WILL DIE, FETT. I WILL PLAY WITH HIM AND THEN I WILL FEED HIM TO MY RANCOR. YOU'VE COLLECTED THE BOUNTY. NOW LEAVE.

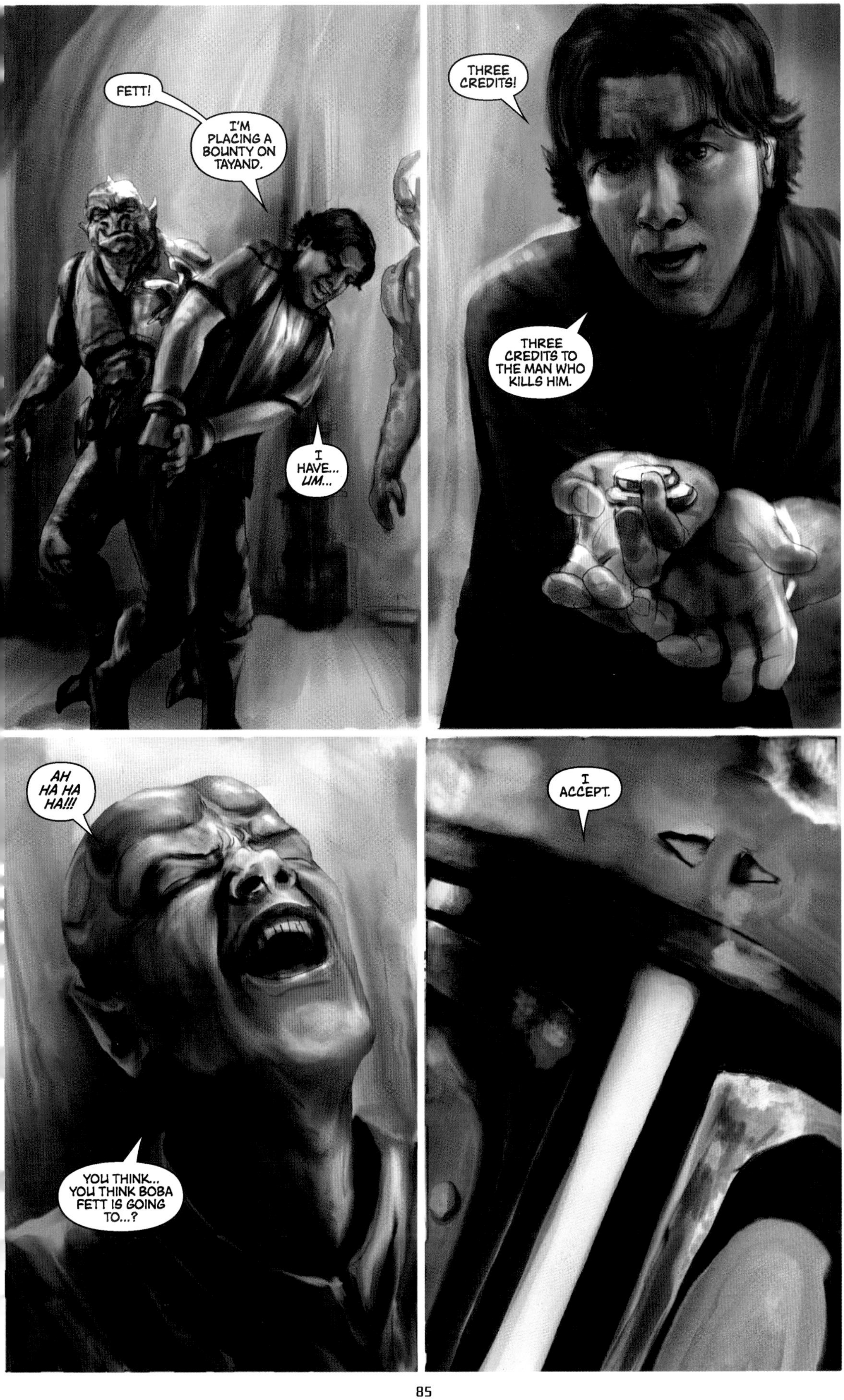
FETT!
I'M PLACING A BOUNTY ON TAYAND.
I HAVE... UM...
THREE CREDITS!
THREE CREDITS TO THE MAN WHO KILLS HIM.
AH HA HA HA!!!
YOU THINK... YOU THINK BOBA FETT IS GOING TO...?
I ACCEPT.

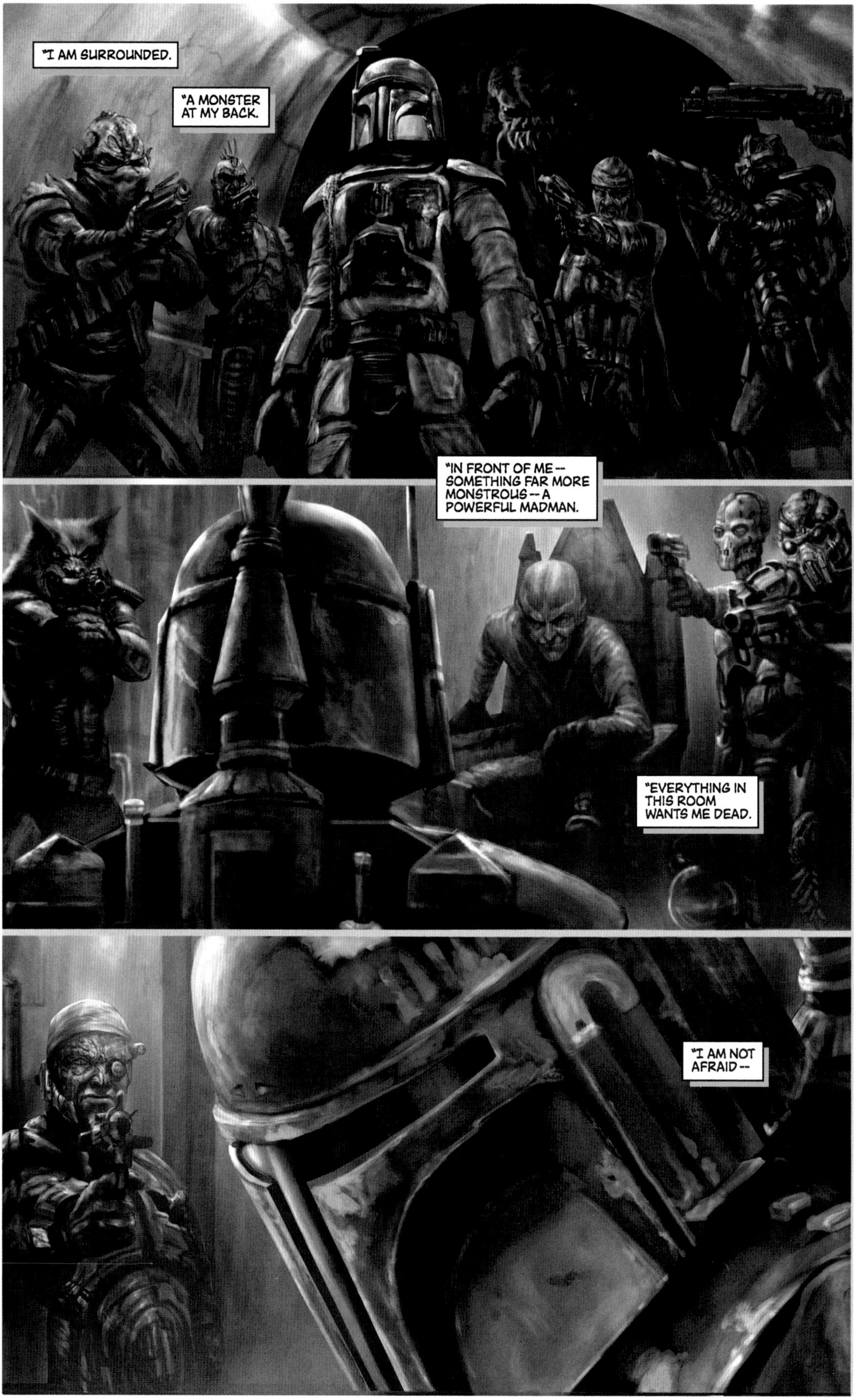

"I AM SURROUNDED.
"A MONSTER AT MY BACK.
"IN FRONT OF ME -- SOMETHING FAR MORE MONSTROUS -- A POWERFUL MADMAN.
"EVERYTHING IN THIS ROOM WANTS ME DEAD.
"I AM NOT AFRAID --

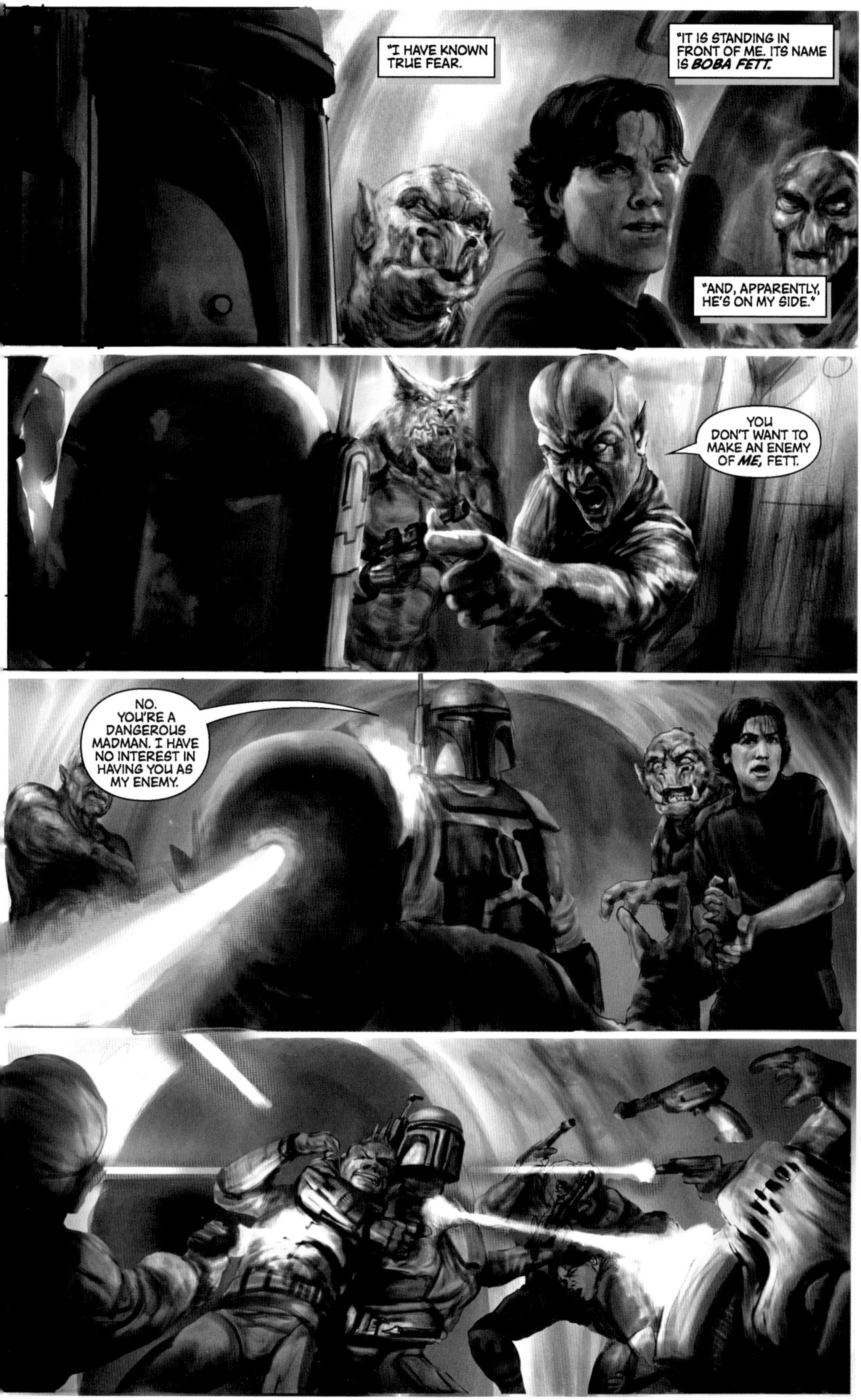
"I HAVE KNOWN TRUE FEAR.
"IT IS STANDING IN FRONT OF ME. ITS NAME IS BOBA FETT.
"AND, APPARENTLY, HE'S ON MY SIDE."
YOU DON'T WANT TO MAKE AN ENEMY OF ME, FETT.
NO. YOU'RE A DANGEROUS MADMAN. I HAVE NO INTEREST IN HAVING YOU AS MY ENEMY.

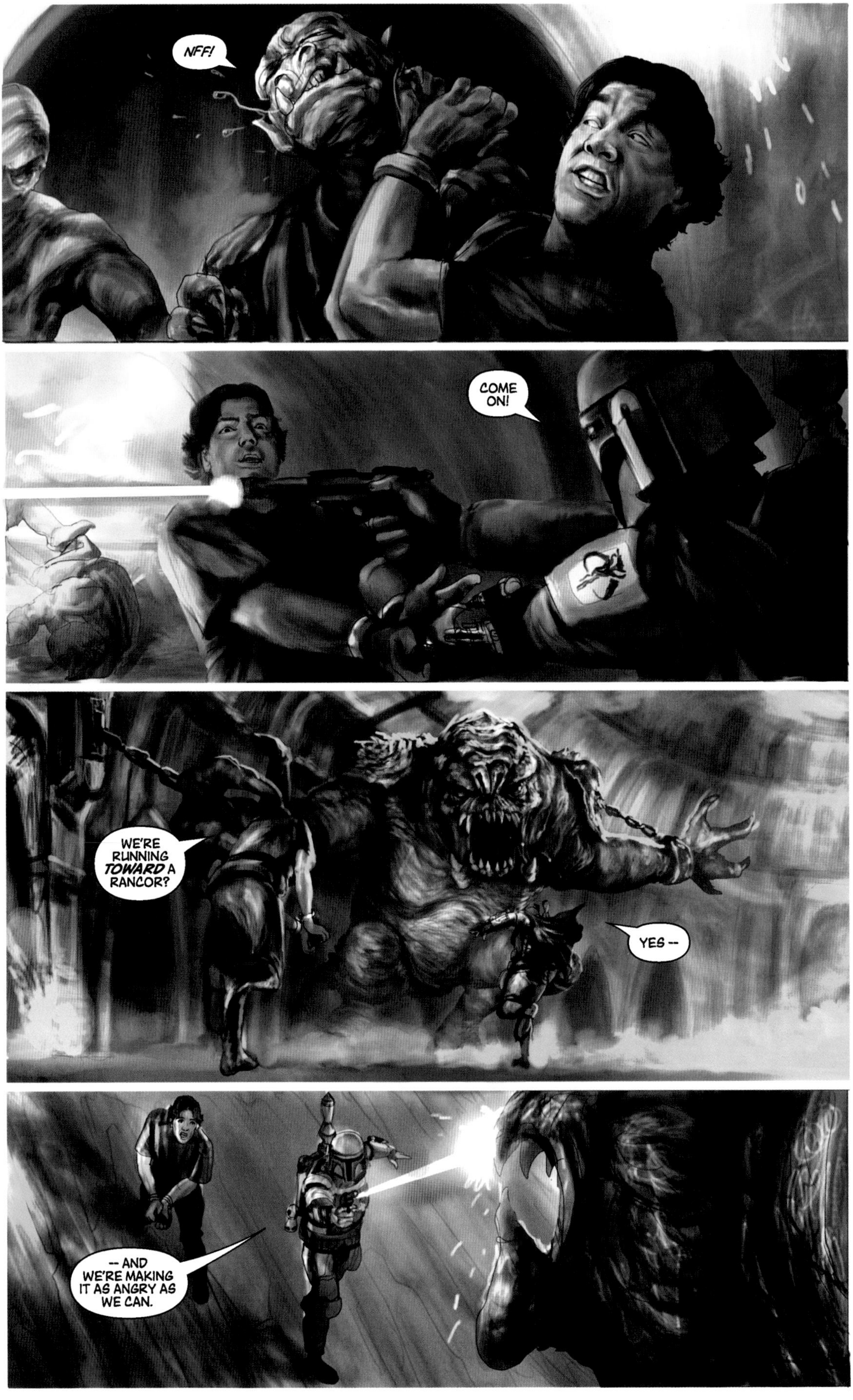

NFF!
COME ON!
WE'RE RUNNING *TOWARD* A RANCOR?
YES --
-- AND WE'RE MAKING IT AS ANGRY AS WE CAN.

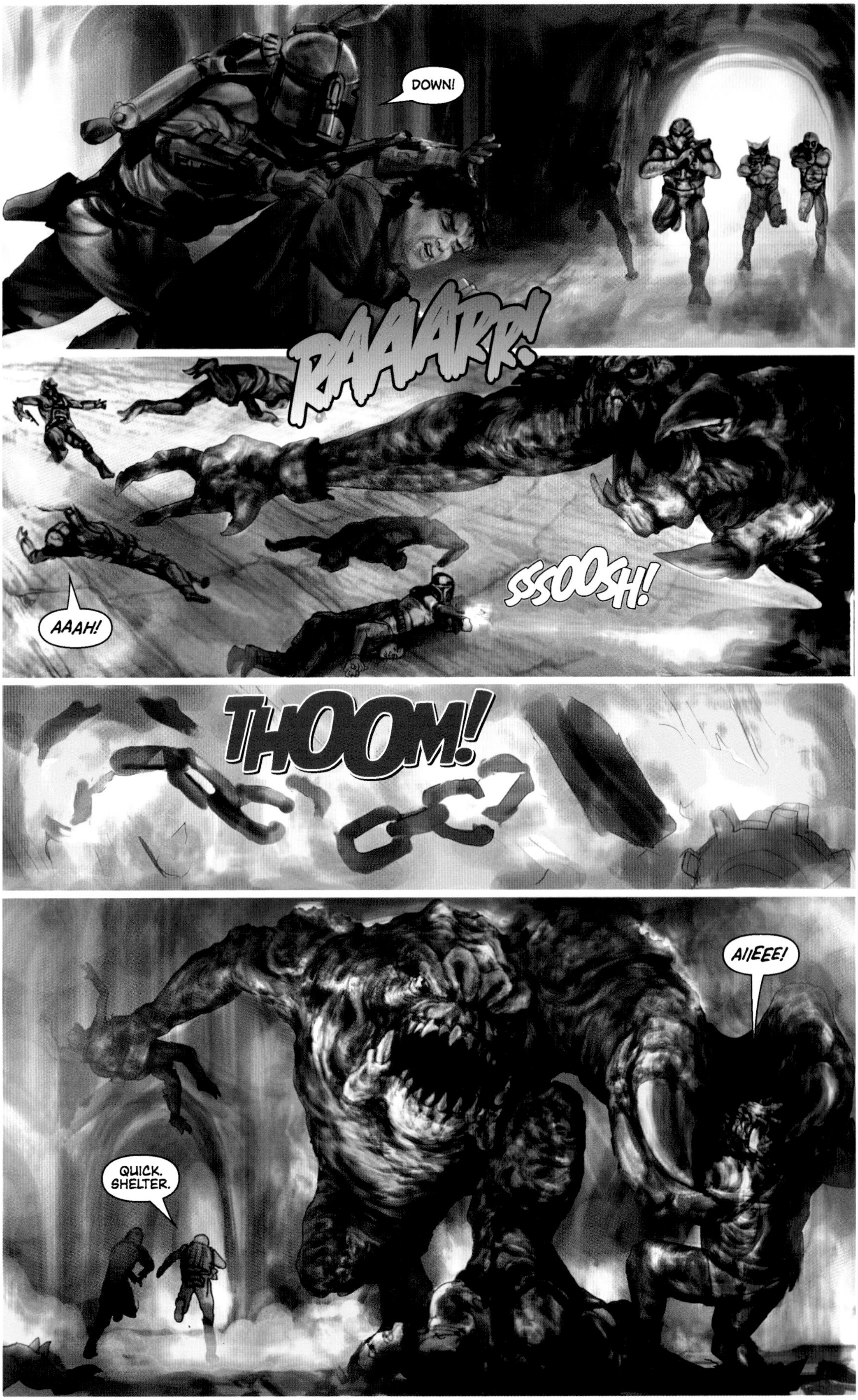
DOWN!
RAAARR!
AAAH!
SSSOOSH!
THOOM!
AIIEEE!
QUICK. SHELTER.

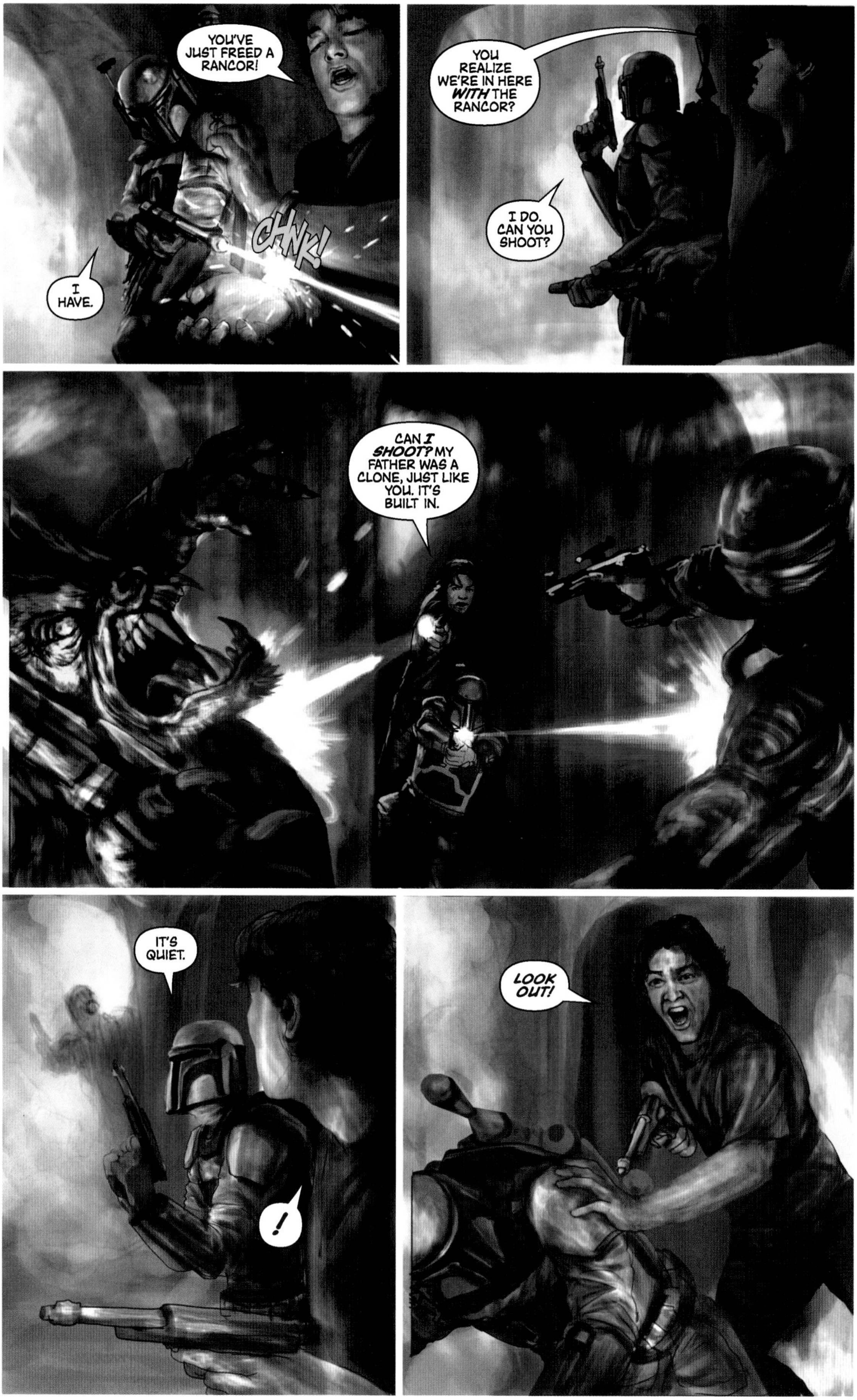
YOU'VE JUST FREED A RANCOR!
CHNK!
I HAVE.
YOU REALIZE WE'RE IN HERE WITH THE RANCOR?
I DO. CAN YOU SHOOT?
CAN I SHOOT? MY FATHER WAS A CLONE, JUST LIKE YOU. IT'S BUILT IN.
IT'S QUIET.
!
LOOK OUT!

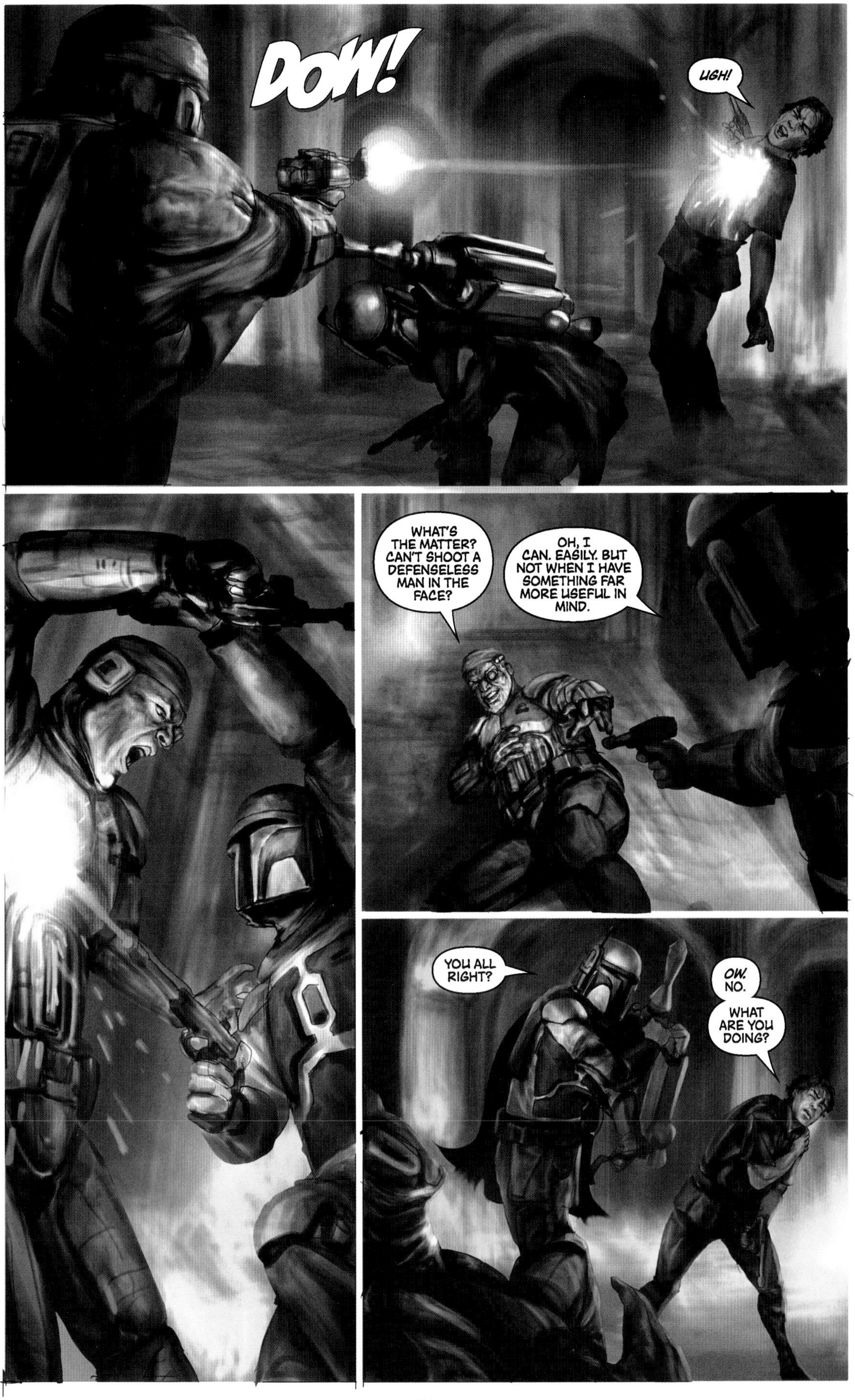
DOW!
UGH!
WHAT'S THE MATTER? CAN'T SHOOT A DEFENSELESS MAN IN THE FACE?
OH, I CAN. EASILY. BUT NOT WHEN I HAVE SOMETHING FAR MORE USEFUL IN MIND.
YOU ALL RIGHT?
OW. NO.
WHAT ARE YOU DOING?

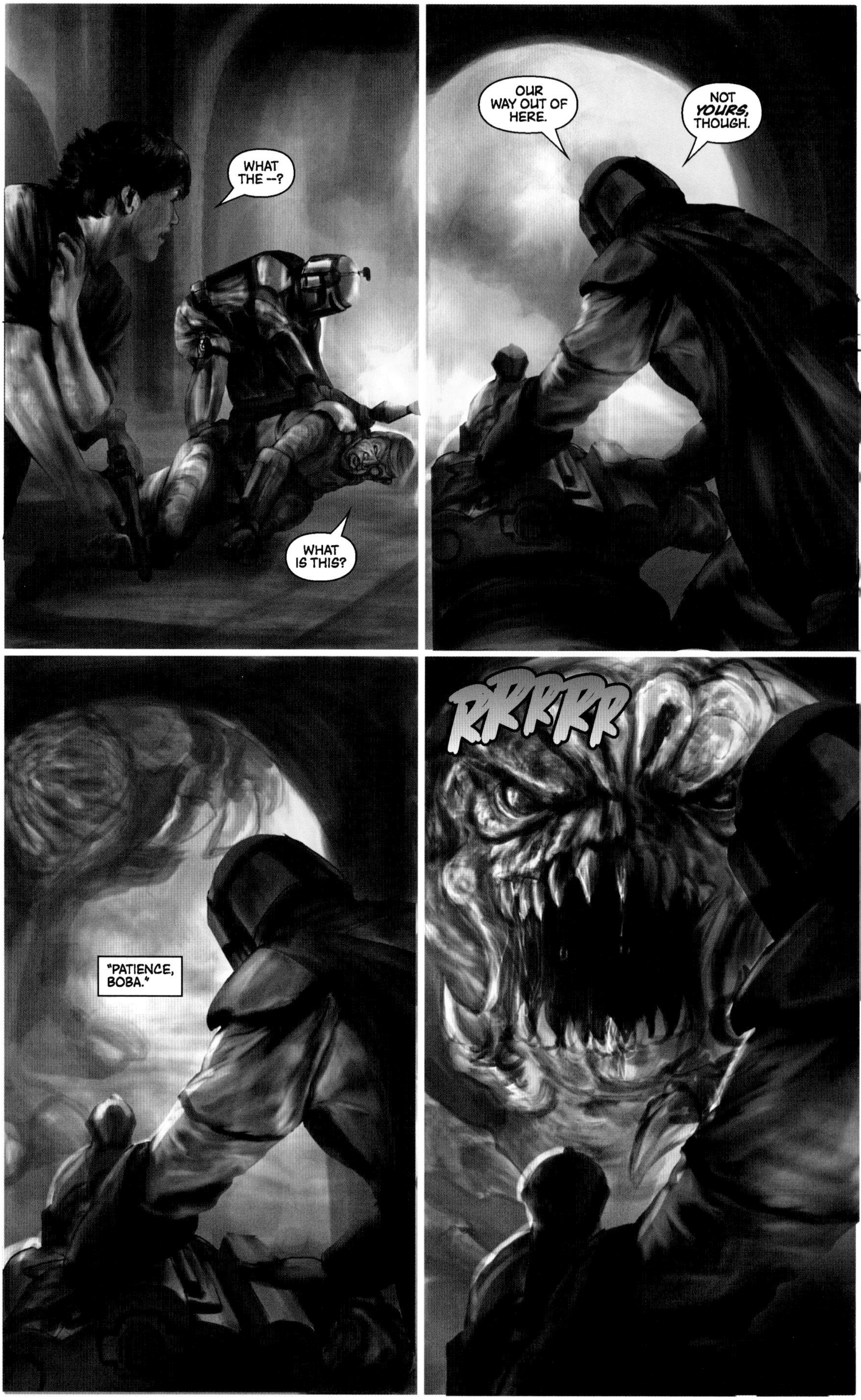
WHAT THE --?
WHAT IS THIS?
OUR WAY OUT OF HERE.
NOT YOURS, THOUGH.
"PATIENCE, BOBA."
RRRRR

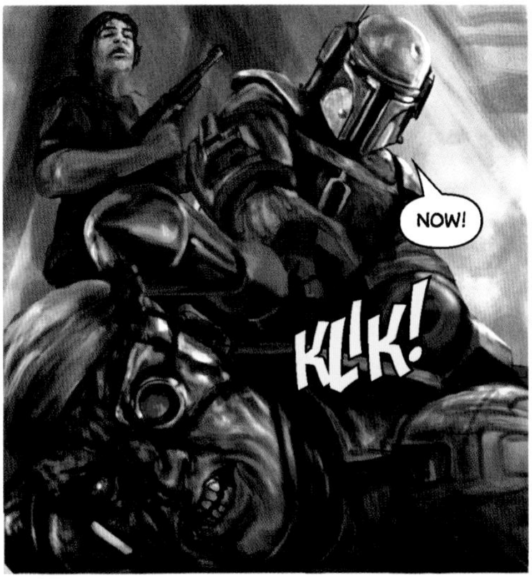
NOW!
KLIK!

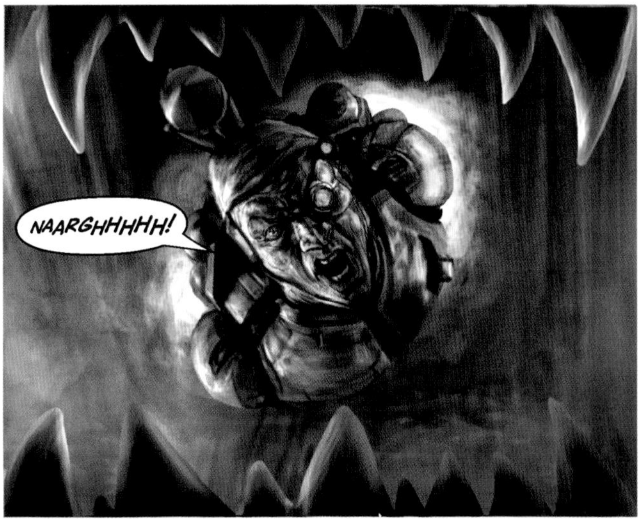
NAARGHHHHH!

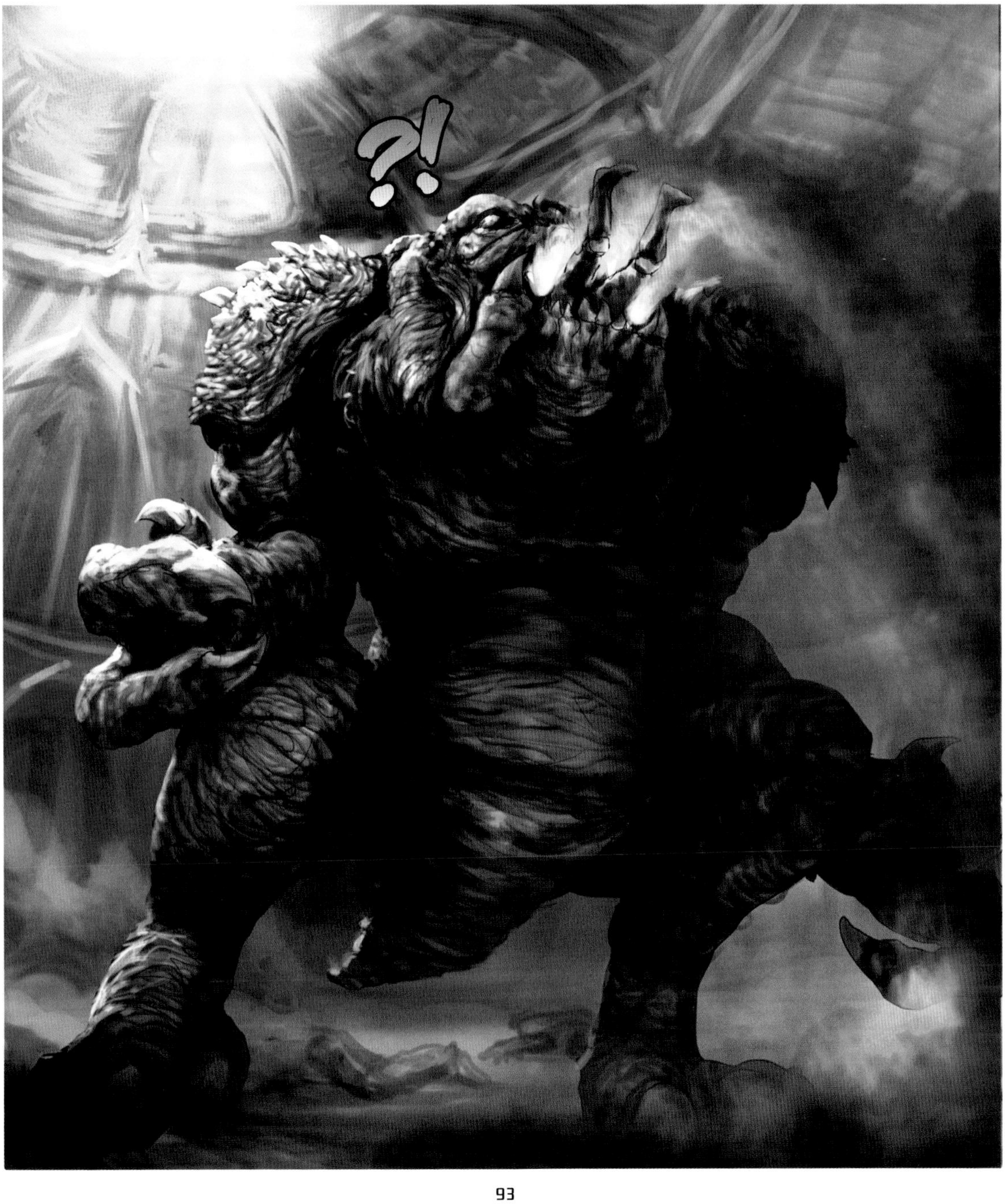
?!

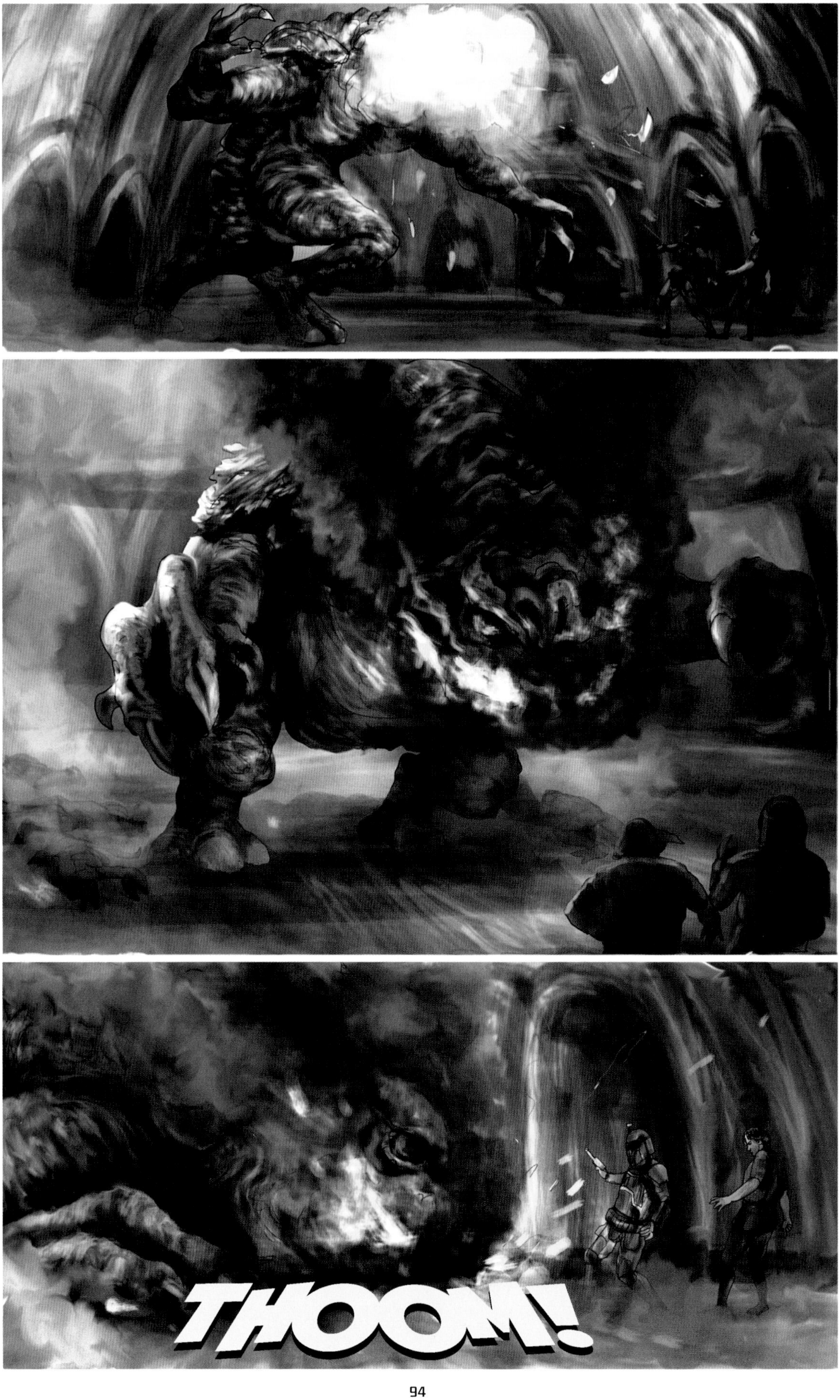
THOOM!

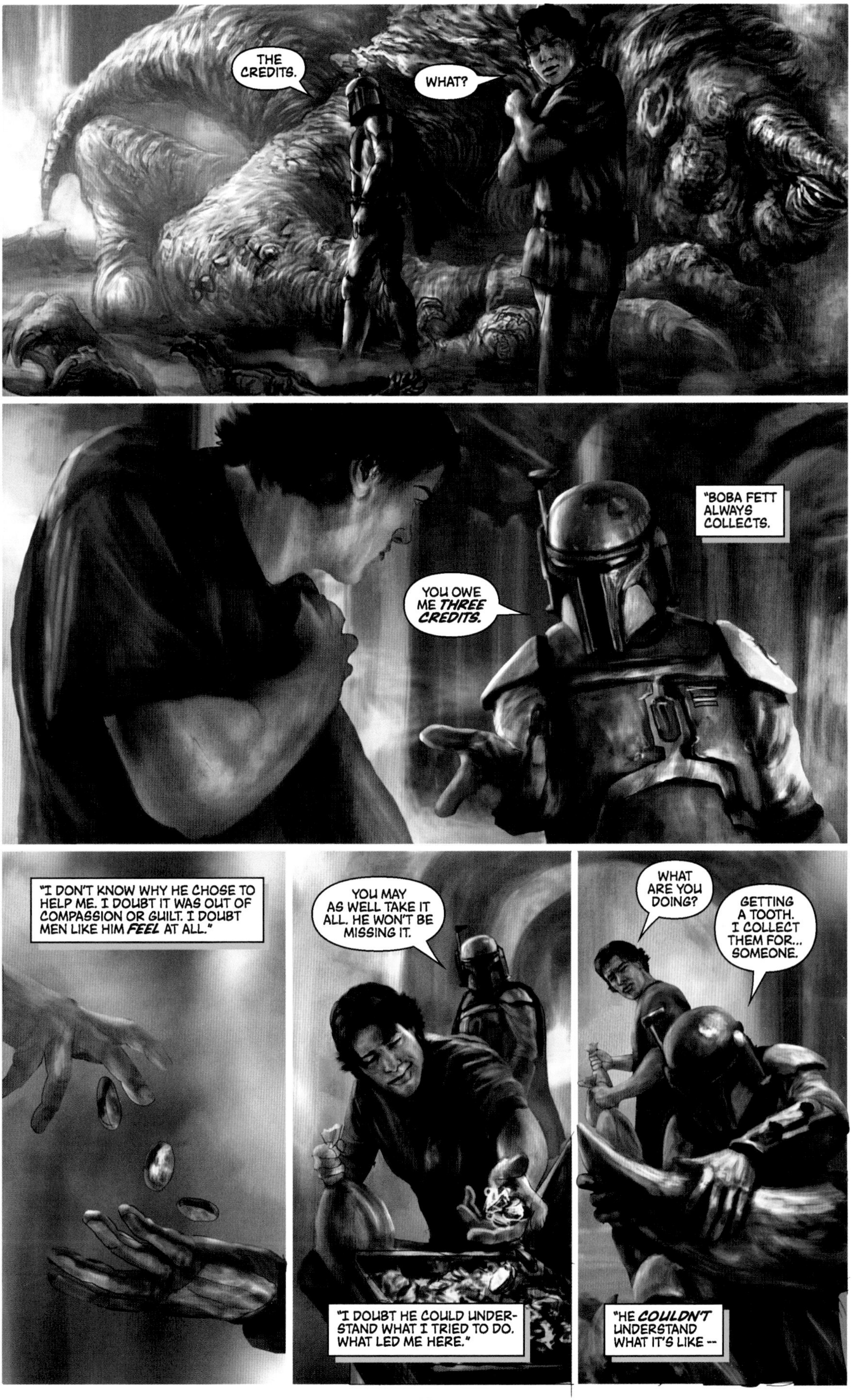
THE CREDITS.
WHAT?
"BOBA FETT ALWAYS COLLECTS.
YOU OWE ME *THREE CREDITS.*
"I DON'T KNOW WHY HE CHOSE TO HELP ME. I DOUBT IT WAS OUT OF COMPASSION OR GUILT. I DOUBT MEN LIKE HIM *FEEL* AT ALL."
YOU MAY AS WELL TAKE IT ALL. HE WON'T BE MISSING IT.
"I DOUBT HE COULD UNDER-STAND WHAT I TRIED TO DO. WHAT LED ME HERE."
WHAT ARE YOU DOING?
GETTING A TOOTH. I COLLECT THEM FOR... SOMEONE.
"HE *COULDN'T* UNDERSTAND WHAT IT'S LIKE --

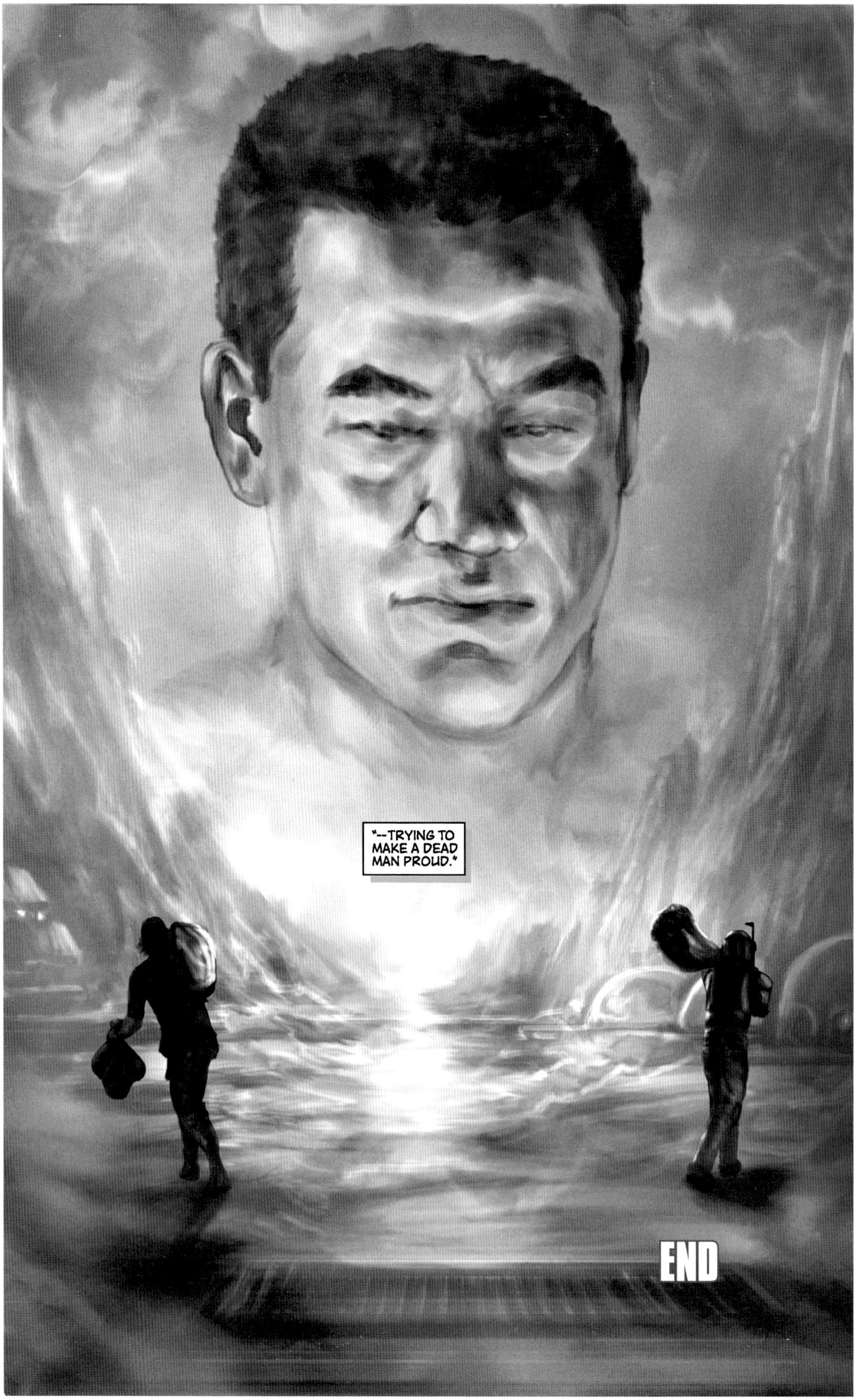
"--TRYING TO MAKE A DEAD MAN PROUD."
END